How to Stay Cool, Calm & Collected When the Pressure's On

How to Stay Cool, Calm & Collected When the Pressure's On

A Stress Control Plan for Businesspeople

John E. Newman, Ph.D.

amacom

American Management Association

This book is available at a special
discount when ordered in bulk quantities.
For information, contact Special Sales Department,
AMACOM, a division of American Management Association,
1601 Broadway, New York, NY 10019.

Library of Congress Cataloging-in-Publication Data

Newman, John E.
  How to stay cool, calm & collected when the pressure's on : a
stress-control plan for businesspeople / John E. Newman.
      p.   cm.
  Includes bibliographical references and index.
  ISBN 978-0-8144-0040-1
  1. Job stress—Management.   2. Success in business.   3. Stress
management.   I. Title.
  HF5548.85.N49   1992
  158.7—dc20   91-40633
                                                                CIP

Printing number

15 16 17 18 19 20

It is with great joy that I dedicate this book
to my wife Barbara and my sons Jeff and Jeremy
for their love and for their magnificent support
of this considerable, long-term effort,
and to my father (Gene Newman, deceased)
and my mother (Opal Newman)
for their love and the solid foundation
they provided me on which to build my life.

Contents

Acknowledgments

I want to express my sincere gratitude to the following inspirational people who have taken the time and effort to share, in a variety of formats, what they have learned in their quest for the secrets of personal effectiveness, health, and happiness: Dr. Karl Albrecht, Dr. Robert Anthony, Dr. Alfred Barrios, Dr. Herbert Benson, Dr. Kenneth Blanchard, Richard Bolles, Claude Bristol, Dr. Leo Buscaglia, Dale Carnegie, Diane Cirincione, Dr. Stephen Covey, Thomas Crum, Peter Drucker, Dr. Wayne Dyer, Alexander Everett, Robert Fritz, Robert Fulghum, Dr. Charles Garfield, Dr. Shad Helmstetter, Napoleon Hill, Tom Hopkins, Dr. Gerald Jampolsky, John-Roger, Dr. Spencer Johnson, Harold Kushner, Ed Foreman, Dr. Jonathan Freedman, David Harp, Dr. Lawrence LeShan, Dr. James Loehr, Og Mandino, Mark McCormack, Peter McLaughlin, Dr. Emmett Miller, Frank Nead, Earl Nightingale, Dr. Norman Vincent Peale, Dr. M. Scott Peck, Dr. Kenneth Pelletier, Tom Peters, Anthony Robbins, Dr. Robert Schuller, Dr. Gini Graham Scott, Jose Silva, W. Clement Stone, Brian Tracy, Dr. Donald Tubesing, Dr. Denis Waitley, Robert Waterman, Jr., and Zig Ziglar. They have contributed immensely to my personal and professional effectiveness, to the overall quality of my life, and to the lives that I have been fortunate to touch.

My thanks to Andrea Pedolsky and Richard Gatjens at AMACOM for their very helpful editorial suggestions and to Jeff Herman, my literary agent, for his crucial role in making this book happen. I want to thank Regina Elinich for her excellent typing of the manuscript, especially of the nearly indecipherable rough drafts.

And my thankful appreciation to my clients for what they

have taught me about the meaning of life, for the opportunity to contribute to their cause, and for making me feel so joyous when they tell me of the wise choices they've made and the wise actions they've taken and of the subsequent positive impact on their effectiveness, health, and happiness!

Introduction

Why You Need a Lifelong Plan for Handling Problems and Stress

This book can be enormously valuable to you—right now and for the rest of your life! Let's face it. If you are a hardworking, dedicated executive, manager, or professional in today's demanding business environment, then there's a very good chance you are seriously undermining your effectiveness, destroying your health, ruining your relationships, and killing the quality of your life *if* you don't know how to approach problems and deal with stress effectively.

The long hours and heavy workload; mergers, layoffs, and restructurings; intense global competition, role ambiguity, or lack of job security; and poor communications and time pressures may be doing you in; not to mention the problems in your family and personal life.

You must take good care of yourself—your body, mind, and spirit—every day to be effective *and* healthy *and* happy. That's the basic premise of this book. The more you neglect yourself, the less able you are to deal with problems and stress, and the less able you are to produce the results you desire most in your life.

Gaining Control of the Way You Handle Problems and Stress

Can you imagine what your life would be like if you could deal with all stressful problems in a way that makes you far more effective, healthier, and happier? Would you be a real star at work? Would you be a better parent? Would you enjoy your personal and social life a lot more? And what other possibilities would open up for you? Promotions? Great times with family and friends? New "personal bests" with respect to your development and performance? Pretty exciting, right?

The ability to control your reaction to a stressful situation is one of the most powerful skills you can ever develop. Many benefits and marvelous opportunities can be yours *if* you can just learn how to approach problems and deal with stress more effectively.

- Imagine yourself being emotionally resilient and bouncing back quickly no matter what pain you experience in life. Imagine turning major setbacks into personal triumphs.
- Imagine yourself being physically stronger, full of energy, and enjoying vibrant health, no longer vulnerable to the physical ravages of stress and strain.
- Imagine yourself being mentally tough and able to focus your energy on achieving your most important goals with a clear head and total concentration, and thus able to produce your desired results much faster.
- Imagine yourself approaching all tough problems in a cool, calm, and collected manner, never letting any problem get you down, including "problem people."
- Imagine yourself happier, truly enjoying your work, your family, yourself, and the world around you. Imagine yourself enjoying each moment of your journey as well as your destination.

Valuable Benefits Desired and Gained by Some of My Clients

You are not alone in your desire to handle stressful situations more effectively. Here are examples of personal effectiveness goals some of my clients have set for themselves and have achieved:

• *Computer operations manager:* "Since the merger, I've been trying to make sure I keep my job. People have been cut and I've got more responsibility with fewer resources to get the job done. I've been working long hours just to stay afloat. I want to learn how to deal with this very stressful situation."

• *A competitive, hard-driving director of marketing:* "I want to deal with my staff and peers in a more respectful, caring, win-win manner instead of jumping to conclusions and ramming my opinions down their throats in angry, emotional outbursts when under pressure."

• *Medical doctor:* "I want to learn how to relax. The hours I put in are ridiculous. When I'm not working, I'm always on call. All the extra work that has to be done to avoid potential malpractice, to practice legally defensible medicine, really makes my blood boil. Dealing with the insurance carriers, my partners and office staff, and all the demands my family put on me is impossible. If I could get out of medicine, I would. I want to learn how to deal with all of this."

• *Vice-president, finance:* "I want to learn how to lead a more balanced, healthier life. I want to spend more time with my family and enjoy a social life but still make significant contributions at work. My marriage is deteriorating. I work long hours and my wife and I are growing apart. When we are together, there's always a lot of arguing. I want to do well in my job *and* save my marriage."

• *A sales professional who makes presentations to high-level executive committees and important industry groups:* "I want to be able to prepare for presentations without worrying so much and getting myself all worked up in anticipation, and I want to make presentations without being so nervous."

• *Manager of engineering department:* "I want to learn how to deal effectively with my boss, who is a real SOB. He's driving me crazy."

• *Research and development scientist:* "I'm a perfectionist. I do excellent work but they say it takes me too long to get things done. The pressure is on for everyone to be more productive. I want to learn how to deal with all the pressure, be more productive, and still be pleased with the quality of my work."

I am happy to report that by using the principles and personal effectiveness skills presented in this book, these people successfully achieved their goals.

Use this Valuable Benefits Checklist to identify the specific benefits *you* want to enjoy as a result of learning how to deal with problems and stress more effectively.

Valuable Benefits Checklist

☐ Greater personal effectiveness at work and at home
☐ Better health, more energy and stamina, more physical resilience to stress
☐ Feel in control and in charge of my life
☐ Feel better about myself, greater self-confidence, high self-esteem
☐ A greatly improved quality of life—more fun, joy, happiness
☐ More enjoyment of my work
☐ A nearly constant state of positive thinking and optimism; elimination of fear, worry, and other types of debilitating negative thinking
☐ The ability to stay clear-headed, thinking and functioning at a high level at all times
☐ Increased ability to channel my energy into productive activity, less wasted time and energy
☐ More patience, more empathetic understanding of others, more compassion, better relationships with people at work, at home, everywhere
☐ A new "I can handle *any* problem" attitude, I'll no longer let problems get me down or destroy me, I'll look forward to tackling problems, I'll replace procrastination with decisiveness and action
☐ The ability to stay focused on creating the results I desire most in my job, family, and personal life
☐ The ability to deal with change in a positive, healthy manner
☐ The ability to stay creative and productive under stress instead of withdrawing or wasting energy on anger and hostility

☐ The ability to see what's going on more clearly, to learn more quickly
☐ A balance between success in my job and a healthy, happy personal life
☐ Being a better spouse, a better parent
☐ Other:_____

The Facts of Life

Problems and stress are facts of life. Your life will always have problems, disappointments, and struggles. That's just the way life is.

"For a long time it had seemed to me that life was about to begin—real life. But there was always some obstacle in the way, some thing to be got through first, some unfinished business, time still to be served, a debt to be paid. Then life would begin. At last it dawned on me that these obstacles were my life."

—Fr. Alfred D'Souza

We All Have Problems

If you think you are the only person with problems or stress, think again. We all have problems of one sort or another. I don't know of anyone who is not grappling with some difficulty in his or her life. Do you?

This includes the most successful people: corporate leaders, top-notch professionals, political leaders, sports heroes, entertainment stars, and religious leaders. And it includes mothers and fathers, managers and workers, brothers and sisters, sons and daughters. It certainly includes all the people you work for, all the people you work with, and all the people who work for you.

We Will Always Have Problems

"Everyday there's always something." How often have you heard that?

Some problems stay with us all our life. Some get solved, some go away. But new problems pop up every day. This also is a fact of life.

We have made monumental strides in developing our civilization. We have solved innumerable problems in nearly every field of human endeavor. But with all this progress, is life any less stressful? Are there fewer problems in the world today, compared to 100 years ago? No. Along with all the problems we have solved, we have discovered many new problems and created more stress.

We will *always* have stressful problems to face, at every age and stage of our life from cradle to grave.

So the fact that you have problems and stress to deal with isn't the real problem. The real problem is failing to take the time to learn how to approach problems and deal *effectively* with stress. In other words, you haven't learned how to take good care of yourself.

Why not learn how to approach problems and deal with stress effectively *now*? Believe me, it's better late than never. It definitely is the smart thing to do.

You Can Handle *Any* Problem That Comes Your Way— If You Have a Plan

This book provides you with a fantastic opportunity to develop a plan for dealing with problems and stress—a Personal Effectiveness Plan that will serve you well—right now and for the rest of your life. It will bring joy to your life by showing you how to take good care of yourself. You'll learn how to approach problems and deal with stress in a way that makes you far more effective, a lot healthier, and a whole lot happier. It will strengthen your ability to handle any difficult situation, and show you how to be *consistently* cool, calm, collected, positive, productive, and healthy, especially when the going gets tough.

I wrote this book because I care about you. And I care about the people you come in contact with and have an impact on (e.g., your spouse, children, mother, father, brothers, sisters, boss, peers, staff, customers).

I have a very strong commitment to you having a great life! I know you want to be as successful, effective, healthy, and happy as you can possibly be. I want that for you, too. I am committed to helping you be precisely that. That's my mission in life.

What's in This Book?

In Part One, you become aware of just how much your current approach to dealing with problems and stress is affecting your success, health, and happiness. You see what's missing in your current approach, and learn the secret to being in control when dealing with problems and stress.

In Part Two, you start developing your Personal Effectiveness Plan by clarifying the kind of life you truly want and the kind of values you want to use to guide your approach to life. This will result in your very own *Command and Control Center*—a frame of reference that will help you make wiser choices every single day.

In Part Three, you have the opportunity to make some wise choices that will definitely help you create the life you want in a cool, calm, collected, positive, productive, and healthy manner. And you will select specific personal effectiveness skills that will support your choices.

In Part Four, you summarize your lifelong Personal Effectiveness Plan and learn how to use it every day.

You Have the Power!

The message of this book is that you have the power to make choices and take action regarding the way you live your life. You always have choices in every situation, no matter how stressful, no matter how tough. Even if you can't do anything about the situation itself, you can always choose how you look at it and respond to it. You can gain enormous control over your life by *consciously choosing* how you look at and respond to problems and stressful situations.

The main point is: *It's your choice!* How you look at and respond to stressful, frustrating, or pressure-packed situations is your choice. You can choose to be hot, angry, fearful, negative, and unproductive, and end up ineffective, a physical and emotional wreck—burned out, seriously ill, or even dead. Or you can choose to be cool, calm, confident, positive, and productive, and go through life being far more effective, much healthier, and a whole lot happier. It's your choice. And the choice you make will determine the *quality* of your life.

This book will put you back in control of your life by showing you how to make wise choices and take wise action. You will come away with a very powerful *overall* approach and *specific* techniques for dealing with problems and stress for the rest of your life. You will even learn *how to deal with most problems before they even happen!* You will be able to say with great confidence, "Whenever I run into a tough problem, especially when the going gets really tough, here's how I'm going to approach it." And you will learn how to "lock onto" the kind of life you truly want and how to create that life with minimum wasted energy and maximum joy.

Rest assured that what I offer you in this book works. *It works. It works. It works.* And it may very well take 15 strokes off your golf game. In fact, you will find you have a much better approach to *everything!*

Take pride in how you approach problems and deal with stress. *Take the time* to learn how to take problems in stride. Do it once, right now via this book, and get it over with. And reap the incredible benefits for the rest of your life.

Having been inspired by many of Earl Nightingale's (founder of the world's largest producer of success-oriented audio-cassette programs) metaphors of success-producing action, I close this introduction with an adaptation of one of his metaphors and with this promise:

> The person who picks up this book and reads it will be a different person. A stronger, more powerful person. A person able to exercise far greater control over success, over health, and over happiness. When the last page of this book is read, the hand that puts the book down on

the table will be a different hand. The person who then stands up and walks out into the world will be a changed person. The entangling webs of self-imposed stress and lack of direction will have fallen away and the way made clear. The person now is able to turn problems into opportunities, stress into productive action, dreams into reality, thoughts into things. So-called fate or exterior circumstances are no longer in command. The person who had been a passenger is now, suddenly, the captain.

YOU MUST TAKE GOOD CARE OF YOURSELF
TO BE EFFECTIVE,
HEALTHY,
AND HAPPY.

Part One

Your Current Approach: What's Missing?

To achieve a breakthrough in how you approach problems, deal with stress, and produce desired results, it's essential that you ask yourself these questions:

* How is your current approach to dealing with problems and stress affecting your effectiveness, health, and happiness?
* What *is* your current approach to dealing with problems and stress? What's working? What's not working? What's missing?
* What is the secret to being in control when dealing with problems and stress?

Once you have answered these questions, you will be in a great position to develop a Personal Effectiveness Plan that makes you far more effective, a lot healthier, and a whole lot happier. Part One helps you see yourself as a powerful person who has choices. You'll learn that you can live in the proactive, create-your-own-life mode instead of a reactive, always-a-victim mode.

How Is Stress Affecting Your Success, Health, and Happiness?

They say a good scare is worth more than good advice. Pain is one way to get your attention, a crisis is another. To illustrate, here is a short story about Larry King (the radio and TV talk-show host) and the heart attack he suffered:

> You have a heart attack, first thing you think is, "I gotta change my life." You know that saying, "Today is the first day of the rest of your life"? Well, you survive a heart attack and that's it: the day after really *is* the first day of the rest of your life. What you don't know is how long that life's gonna be. All of a sudden, you gotta deal with the fact that you *are* going to die one of these days. Death becomes real. And if death is real, then you absolutely have to make the most of what time you've got.
>
> In a way, if you have a heart attack and survive, you're ahead of people who don't have a heart attack—not that I'd wish this experience on anyone! But going through this forces you to really *think* about your life as almost nothing else does. It forces you to consider what's important and what isn't. And it gives you the chance to make changes and adjustments that you might otherwise never even realize you might want to make.*

*Larry King with B. D. Colen, *Mr. King, You're Having a Heart Attack* (New York: Delacorte Press, 1989).

In today's turbulent business environment, all ambitious and hardworking executives, managers, and professionals face a constant barrage of problems and stress in their jobs and in their personal lives. Dealing with these pressures and frustrations is a major problem for most of them, including the brightest and most well-intentioned among them.

How are you handling the problems and stress in *your* life?

An executive once said to me, "I'm juggling about a dozen very important balls in the air. I enjoy the excitement and the challenge, but I'm working sixteen hours a day. I'm overweight. My blood pressure and cholesterol levels are high. I smoke and drink unthinkingly. I'm arguing more with my spouse, who also works full-time at a very demanding job. My teenage daughter was in a serious car accident two months ago. If I continue leading the stressful life I'm living now, it's going to kill me."

A manager from another corporation told me the uncertainty and insecurity of a recent merger, repeated reorganizations and downsizings, and the ever-increasing pressure to "do more with less" was finally getting to him. Formerly a strong, vibrant person, he now was experiencing health problems and was becoming disillusioned. He wanted some way to get off the "fast-moving treadmill," to regain his health and his normally positive outlook.

Let's face it. If you are a motivated, conscientious executive, manager, or professional, there's a good chance you are undermining your effectiveness, destroying your health, and ruining the quality of your life if you *don't* deal effectively with stress and pressure.

The American Institute of Stress reports that 66 percent of all visits to primary-care physicians are for stress-related disorders. Stress is a heavy contributor to heart disease, cancer, respiratory distress, and many other life-threatening illnesses. Job-related stress costs American industry between $100 and $300 billion a year in absenteeism, poor service, lost productivity, mistakes and accidents, medical insurance, and workers' compensation claims. Insurance companies say that stress has become the number-one employee health hazard.

Not a week goes by without a major business paper or

magazine article on the destructive pervasiveness of uncontrolled stress at work. A Wharton School of Business professor stated that the inability to deal with stress is the foremost problem in corporate America. A number of high-level executives agree wholeheartedly.

What painful consequences are *you* experiencing because of your current approach to dealing with problems and stress? Uncontrolled stress can affect your body, mind, and behavior in many ways and will subsequently affect your work, health, and happiness. Uncontrolled stress can affect your production *capability* as well as the results you produce.

Wake-Up Call!

Is whatever you are doing at work worth dying for? Or worth sacrificing the quality of your life? Wake up to what stress is doing to you. Use the following Wake-Up Call Checklist to clarify the impact stress is having on your life. Be honest with yourself. You're doing this for *your* benefit.

Wake-Up Call Checklist

How stress is affecting my body and physical health:
- [ ] Tense, tight muscles, especially neck, shoulders, or jaw
- [ ] Headaches
- [ ] Back pain
- [ ] Elevated blood pressure
- [ ] Numbness and tingling in limbs
- [ ] Heartburn, hyperacidity, indigestion
- [ ] Colitis, peptic ulcers
- [ ] Difficulty breathing, shortness of breath, asthma
- [ ] Chest pain, angina
- [ ] Allergies, frequent colds
- [ ] Skin rash
- [ ] Dry mouth, lump in throat
- [ ] Chronic fatigue, exhaustion, low energy
- [ ] Weakened immune system

☐ Overweight, out of shape
☐ Trouble getting to sleep or staying asleep
☐ Cold hands or feet
☐ Diabetic reactions
Note: This is a short list; stress can affect *any* system in your body.

How stress is affecting my mental capabilities and emotional health:

☐ Anxious, nervous
☐ Depressed, don't enjoy life, no enthusiasm, disillusioned
☐ Emotionally drained, mentally strained
☐ Personally devalued, broken spirit
☐ Excessively frustrated with self or others
☐ Impatient, overly demanding
☐ Feelings of guilt, shame, blame self, criticize self
☐ Irritable, bad tempered, have emotional outbursts
☐ Hypersensitive to criticism
☐ Moody
☐ Low self-esteem, feel inadequate, low self-acceptance, shaky self-confidence
☐ Feel insecure, bewildered, numbed or nearly paralyzed by uncertainty
☐ Fearful, scared
☐ Can't recognize and address problems
☐ Nervous, fidgeting, can't keep still
☐ Lonely, feel alienated
☐ Worry a lot, negative thinking
☐ Feel hopeless, feel helpless, can't visualize a positive future
☐ Feel panicky
☐ Cry easily, emotions on surface
☐ Can't concentrate, forgetful
☐ Indecisive
☐ Difficult getting out of bed in morning
☐ Cynical, pessimistic, negative, sarcastic
☐ Can't turn off certain stressful thoughts or feelings

□ Feel overwhelmed, overtaxed, overloaded, overcommitted
□ Have difficulty adjusting to change
□ No sense of humor, don't laugh much anymore
□ Feel driven by "musts," "shoulds," "gottas," and other perfectionistic or approval-seeking self-talk
□ Dissatisfied with job or career
□ Have trouble letting go of a major disappointment
□ Feel out of control
□ Find it difficult to bounce back from setbacks
□ Inattentive to details
□ Hold everything in, don't share my problems, don't express my feelings
□ Can't think clearly, reduced creativity
□ Feel victimized—"Why does this always happen to me?"
□ Not happy with the overall quality of my life

How stress is affecting my behavior and personal effectiveness:

□ Job performance is deteriorating or not what it could be
□ Unable to channel energy into productive actions
□ Overeat, lost my appetite, don't take time to eat or to eat right
□ Drink too much alcohol, rely on alcohol "fix" (caution: denials of this are characteristic of alcoholics)
□ Depend on other drugs or chemicals
□ Smoke excessively
□ Avoid people, withdraw
□ Impaired speech
□ Nervous behavior (e.g., bite nails, pace, fidget, can't keep still)
□ Avoid confronting problems
□ Jump from one unimportant task to another
□ Counterproductive compulsive or ritualistic actions
□ Increased accidents or injuries
□ Increased errors or mistakes

☐ Always in a hurry, pressed for time
☐ Procrastinate, have trouble getting going
☐ Make bad decisions, fail to make decisions
☐ Criticize, blame, or ridicule others, put others down
☐ Have difficulty meeting commitments or completing tasks
☐ Watch TV excessively
☐ Take tranquilizers
☐ Lost interest in appearance
☐ Surrendering my life, in quiet desperation, to the demands of others
☐ Abuse others
☐ Frequently late or absent
☐ Less effective, less efficient, less productive
☐ Don't get along with others; relationships with people are deteriorating
☐ Overreact or underreact to stressful situations
☐ Do self-defeating, nonconfronting things to forget my distress (e.g., shopping sprees, eating binges)
☐ Try to do things perfectly
☐ Am addicted to work (e.g., always working late or bringing work home)
☐ Try to be "superhuman"—scramble like crazy to have it all, do it all, be it all
☐ Don't communicate effectively with people or at all
☐ Overly competitive or hard-driving, even in noncompetitive situations
☐ Must fill every moment with achievement-oriented behavior
☐ Set unrealistic and often unnecessary deadlines
☐ Engage in available but not really productive activity just to stay busy
☐ Become hostile when a person or thing gets in the way of achieving my goal
☐ Drive erratically
☐ Devote too much time to one area of my life and neglect other important areas

Note: Stress can affect *any* behavior you engage in.

Your Conclusions

Take a look at the items you checked. Is stress affecting your success? Your effectiveness? Your health? Your happiness? Is whatever you are doing at work worth dying for? Or worth sacrificing your enjoyment of life?

The number of items you checked is less important than doing something about your situation. If you are experiencing any significant physical, emotional, or behavioral problems, get professional attention immediately. It's not normal to go through a roll or two of antacids every day. It's not necessary to take out your frustration on your family. Yes, people do have heart attacks. Whatever your situation, quit procrastinating and take action now. As one of my clients said, "I wish I knew this stuff *before* I had my heart attack!" A visit to your doctor, corporate medical department, or employee assistance person is a good place to start.

If your symptoms are not yet serious and are amenable to self-help efforts, then read on!

Your Future: Will Your Star Be Shining or Burned Out?

Give yourself a really good scare. Given the current drift in your job, health, and relationships, what are things going to look like for you in the next five to ten years? If you keep living the way you are and don't make any adjustments in how you approach the problems and stress in your life, what will your life be like in five years? In ten years?

* How effective and productive will you be?
* How successful?
* How healthy?
* What will your relationships be like?
* What will the overall quality of your life be like?
* How happy will you be?

Is it clear that, if you *don't* learn how to deal with problems and stress *effectively*, you are going to kill the goose that's laying the golden eggs? At best, you will undermine your effectiveness, health, and personal relationships and make it virtually impossible to enjoy any success you may achieve.

In the next chapter, you will look at how you are currently approaching problems and stress. The checklist in this chapter probably showed you there's something wrong. Why isn't your current approach working?

HERE'S A LINE THAT'LL KILL YOU:
I DON'T HAVE TIME TO LEARN HOW TO DEAL
WITH PROBLEMS AND STRESS EFFECTIVELY.

2

What Is Your Current Approach? What's Missing?

"Life is a series of problems. To confront them is often painful; yet it is only through solving problems that we grow . . . and give meaning to our lives. Many of us try to avoid our problems and the emotional suffering they involve, and this tendency is the primary basis of all mental illness."

—*M. Scott Peck, M.D.*, The Road Less Traveled

Since a constant flow of problems is a fact of life, it seems appropriate to have a really effective *approach* for dealing with the problems, right? What *is* your approach? How do you handle the problems, pressures, frustrations, rejections, setbacks, and disappointments in your life? What's your approach for dealing with events that don't go your way or attacks on your self-esteem?

You do have an approach, although you may not have given it much thought. When presented with a problem, you may automatically go into your this-is-how-I-deal-with-problems routine without consciously knowing what it is. It seems the most popular approaches for dealing with problems and stress don't take care of the problems and usually have undesirable side effects. Examples are:

- Not confronting the problem
- Drinking alcohol, taking drugs
- Eating too much, especially sweets
- Lashing out at others, displacing anxiety and anger onto other people
- Passively watching TV for hours

* Withdrawing physically or psychologically
* Not communicating with others
* Engaging in antisocial or violent behavior
* Leading a life of quiet desperation
* Screaming and yelling
* Sitting and stewing
* Worrying

What is your approach to dealing with problems and stress? Consider both your approach to everyday problems and to really stressful, high-pressure, and unbelievably frustrating situations. What do you do? Say? Think? Feel? Try to get someone else's opinion, too. Ask your peers, subordinates, spouse, friends, or children.

How effective is your approach? Is it helping you get what you want out of life or making things worse? How healthy is it? Your responses to the Wake-Up Call Checklist in Chapter 1 certainly shone the flashlight on this matter!

Maybe this is a good time to try something different. If you are not happy with your current approach, then there is a very good chance it is missing the following three factors:

1. Full use of the incredible power you have to influence how you live your life. (I address this in this chapter.)
2. A basic understanding of the real cause (and preventer) of stress. (I address this in Chapter 3.)
3. A concrete, comprehensive, organized, easy-to-use, lifelong plan for approaching problems and dealing with stress. (I address this in Parts Two, Three, and Four.)

Your Incredible Power

There is a better way to live. Choice! The key is choice. You have options. You need not spend your life wallowing in failure, ignorance, grief, poverty, shame, and self-pity. But, hold on! If this is true, then why have so many among us apparently elected to live in that manner? The answer is obvious. Those who live in unhappy failure have never exercised their options for a better way of life because they have never been aware that they had any choices!

——Og Mandino, The Choice

Did you know that you have at your immediate disposal exactly what you need to gain more control over the problems and stress in your life, and thus over your health, happiness, and effectiveness? Did you know that everyone has this secret weapon, but very few people are aware of it, let alone use it purposefully? That secret weapon is *your power to make choices and take action.* You have the power to make conscious choices regarding the way you live your life and the power to take action that supports those choices. This is without a doubt your most valuable weapon in gaining more control over your life.

**YOUR SECRET WEAPON:
YOUR POWER TO
MAKE CHOICES
AND
TAKE ACTION!**

The guiding principle of this "make choices and take action" approach to dealing with problems and stress is: *control what you can control.*

This principle is based on three facts:

1. You can't always control what happens to you in life. You can some of the time. You can't some of the time.
2. You can always control how you look at and respond to what happens to you.
3. Therefore, you always have *some control,* if not in creating the event, then in how you look at it and respond to it.

Now look at this. If you replace the word *control* with the words *choose, choose,* and *choice,* you get this:

1. You can't always choose what happens to you in life. You can some of the time. You can't some of the time.
2. You can always choose how you look at and respond to what happens to you.
3. Therefore, you always have some choice, if not in creating the event, then in how you look at it and respond to it.

So when you make conscious choices about how you look at and deal with situations, you are controlling what you can control. You are exercising the power you *do* have over your life—the power you *always* have in every situation.

For example, how you look at problems and stressful situations is your choice. You can *choose* to be hot, angry, fearful, negative, and unproductive (and end up ineffective, a physical and emotional wreck, or burned out, seriously ill, or even dead). Or you can *choose* to be cool, calm, collected, positive, and productive in those situations (and go through life far more effective, much healthier, and a whole lot happier). It's your choice!

Most people are not aware that they can choose how to look at and deal with difficult situations, that they have choices. They often respond unconsciously to problems with an automatic, stressful reaction that, at best, is ineffective and, at worst, is counterproductive.

You can consciously choose how you *look at* problems.
You can consciously choose how you *deal with* problems.

A Call to Action!

Note carefully that both elements—making conscious choices and taking action—are essential for an effective approach to dealing with the problems and stress in your life. Making choices about how you want to live your life without taking actions that support those choices gives you nothing but more problems, more frustration, and more stress.

The realization that *you* have the power to make conscious choices regarding the way you live your life and to take actions that support your choices, gives rise to a tremendous feeling of personal power! And by using this incredible power more often when facing the problems and stress in your life, you can gain *enormous* control over your life and be far more effective, healthier, and happier.

```
╭───────────────────────────────────────────────╮
┊                                                 ┊
┊        MAKING CHOICES + TAKING ACTION           ┊
┊            = BEING IN CONTROL                   ┊
┊            = PERSONAL POWER                     ┊
┊                                                 ┊
╰───────────────────────────────────────────────╯
```

So start using your incredible power. Start making choices and taking action! Start making *wiser* choices with respect to your effectiveness, health, and happiness, and start *taking action* that supports your choices. If you are looking for someone who can make a major difference in your life, look in the mirror.

Too busy? If you are a hardworking, dedicated person who just doesn't have time to learn how to deal with problems and stress more effectively, I can tell you right now that there will never be a "good time" to do so. You will always be too busy. You will always have more important things to do. That is, until you lose your health, until your spouse demands a divorce, or until you lose your job.

Learning how to deal with problems and stress *is* important. Damn important. Make the time. Take the time. You'll be very glad you did. Don't mess with stress! It can very definitely kill you.

You can consciously choose how you approach and deal with the problems and stress in your life, or you can choose, by default, to let problems and stress control you. It's your choice! And the choice you make will determine, to a large extent, the quality of your life. Take charge. You have the power. Start calling your own plays. Start making choices and taking action.

```
╭───────────────────────────────────────────────╮
┊                                                 ┊
┊              IT'S YOUR CHOICE!                  ┊
┊                                                 ┊
╰───────────────────────────────────────────────╯
```

3

The Key to Being In Control

"There is nothing either good or bad but thinking makes it so."

—*William Shakespeare*, Hamlet

As suggested in Chapter 2, one thing that is probably missing in your current approach to dealing with stress is a basic understanding of the *real* cause of your stress. This chapter will provide you with that understanding, and thereby, allow you to deal with stress quickly and decisively right at its source.

What Stress Is and Where Stress Is

Stress is the feeling you experience when you perceive a gap between what you want and what you have. The bigger the gap and the more important the issue is to you, the greater the potential for stress. In other words:

(Want − have) × (importance to you) = stress potential.

Here are some examples of such gaps:

You want:	You have:
A secure job	A merger and downsizing
Good health	A painful ulcer
To do good work	A boss who is never satisfied
Good relationships	Strained relationships with family members
Nice weather	Lousy weather

This feeling of stress is really a complex emotional, mental, and physiological reaction. It's an *energizing reaction* that activates (and puts a strain on) many of the body's systems. There's a body-wide state of arousal: adrenaline and other hormones are released, heart rate and blood pressure increase, breathing becomes rapid, muscles tighten, acid is pumped into the stomach, and certain brain functions are turned on while others are turned off.

Note that stress is something that happens entirely *inside* you. Stress is not "out there"! It is an internal reaction caused by your perception or interpretation of what is out there. Your stress reaction is created between your ears (i.e., in your mind) and experienced in your body and mind.

Stress is energy! Your perception of a gap between what you want and what you have creates energy (the energizing stress reaction)! So the result of this complex reaction is a buildup of energy inside you. What's important to know is that you need to do something with that energy buildup or it will do something to you.

What Stress, Problems, and the Chance of a Lifetime Have in Common

A problem can also be defined as a perceived gap between what you want and what you have. And the bigger the perceived gap and the more important the issue, the greater the potential for a problem. What stress and problems have in common is a perceived gap between what you want and what you have.

It is *important* to realize that a gap is just a gap. What makes the gap stressful is your perceiving it as stressful. What makes the gap a problem is your perceiving it as a problem. You determine what the gap means by the label or meaning you attach to it. You can label it anything you want. For example, you can call a gap a problem, stress, the chance of a lifetime, a personal challenge, a great opportunity, a disaster, rejection, pressure, a failure, a setback, frustration, a headache, exciting, or anything else you choose to call it. Look at the examples of the gaps at the beginning of this chapter and see how you can make any of these labels "fit" each example.

Since the world was not designed to your exact specifications (oh, shucks), there are lots of gaps between what you want and what you have. There always will be. Some of these gaps will be important, and you will label them as stressful or as problems or opportunities, and you will deal with them. Some of them you will ignore, while some you will learn to live with. The point is, they are all gaps, and what you label them and how you deal with them is your choice. This is part of the key to being in control.

Your Optimal Stress Level

Stress can either help or hinder your personal effectiveness. The relationship usually looks like Figure 1. As your stress level increases, your personal effectiveness increases. But when the stress level passes your optimal stress level, your personal effectiveness deteriorates. This means that stress is good for you when it makes you more alert and energized, and leads to concentrated effort and high levels of performance.

I'm sure you have done some of your best work under

Figure 1. Levels of stress and personal effectiveness.

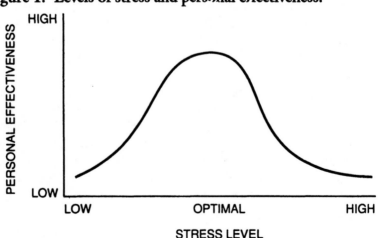

pressure or in a heightened state of arousal. That's what "getting up for the game" is all about. These good effects of stress happen when the energy build up is controlled, focused, and used well on problem solving or goal achievement. For example, when you get hungry, there is a gap between what you want (food) and what you currently have (no food). That gap creates stress, a reaction that energizes you to take action to close the gap (obtain food).

But stress can be bad for you when it makes you feel churned up inside, tense, confused, unable to concentrate, and out of control; and it results in poor performance, illness, or death. These bad effects happen when the energy is uncontrolled, excessive, and used poorly. You are not able to focus it on problem solving or goal achievement. This is the problem with too much stress. It keeps you from creating the results you want in your job, family, and personal life. It makes you lose control over what you are trying to accomplish.

This basic relationship between stress level and personal effectiveness suggests that one of your goals might be to become more aware of your *optimal stress level*, or the amount of stress (arousal) that helps you achieve a high level of personal effectiveness. This is similar to tuning a stringed instrument. Not enough tension (i.e., stress) on the string yields poor performance. Too much tension on the string also yields poor performance and may break the string. The optimal amount of tension produces beautiful music! Increasing your awareness of your optimal stress level and consciously "tuning" your stress level so that it's consistently in the optimal range is another key to being in control.

The amount of stress optimal for high performance varies from person to person. For example, one person might perform best when working at a low arousal level (at a turtle's pace), while another might perform best at a high arousal level (at the speed of a racehorse).

Are you a racehorse, bristling with energy and *needing* to run all out every day in order to be effective? Or are you a turtle, *needing* a slower, more deliberate pace to be most effective? Or something in between? If you are a racehorse and are expected to perform like a turtle, you're going to have problems. If you are a turtle and are expected to perform like a racehorse, you're in deep trouble. Trying to operate at a stress level higher or lower than your optimal range just won't work for very long. The relationship between stress and your health and happiness seems to be quite similar, with optimal health and happiness associated with your optimal stress level.

Acute vs. Chronic Stress

Most people are aware of the rapid emotional and physiological impact of an *acute* stress experience, but they are not aware of the slower cumulative effect of long periods of constant stress.

Every time your body produces the stress reaction, it puts a strain on your system and leads to physical and emotional wear and tear. If you are always in a state of stress, this constant wear and tear can cause you to burn out and break down physically and emotionally. Like racing a car nonstop at high speed, you may get away with it for a while. But at some point, like the race car, you will either run out of gas or one of your internal systems will break down.

The five phases of stress show what can happen as your stress level builds up and continues to rise unchecked over a long period of time.

1. *Gearing up*. The initial energizing reaction gears you up for action. You're excited. Your muscles are charged, your perception acute. All systems are go.
2. *Peak performance*. You channel that energy. You are focused on your goal and you make things happen. You have a positive, high feeling. You are intense.
3. *Using up*. If you remain in high gear, your mind starts to wander, your muscles tighten, and you can feel the strain on your system. You're tired. Your ability to communicate well dwindles, as does your energy supply. Illness may set in at this point.
4. *Running down*. If you continue operating under constant stress with no breaks, no time for recuperating, then your physical and mental states continue to deteriorate.

You may have impaired judgment and more severe stomach, bowel, or cardiovascular problems. Chemical dependence and inappropriate behavior are common. Chronic fatigue may also begin.

5. *Exhaustion or burnout.* Your energy reserves move toward depletion. You feel totally exhausted, emotionally and physically. You become disillusioned; you devalue yourself and your spirit collapses. Severe depression is not uncommon.

As you can see, a long period of constant stress is very dangerous. It's not to be taken lightly. Such chronic stress can lead to serious illness, severe personal ineffectiveness, and death. Unfortunately, "long periods of constant stress" almost defines life in the corporate world and in professional practices today. If you lack good stress-management skills, it is very easy to get trapped in a destructive, vicious cycle of poor responses to stress, and this can be deadly! So, another part of the key to being in control when dealing with constant problems and stress is recognizing when your approach is not working well and taking corrective action *before* you get caught in your ineffective approach. (In Part Three, I will show you how to break the vicious, downward-spiraling cycle of constant stress on a *daily* basis.)

Individual Differences

People differ considerably in how they experience stress and in how they deal with it. What I see as stressful may not bother you at all. How Maureen deals with the layoff may be quite different than how Sally deals with it. Some people are able to handle several demanding situations at the same time and stay cool, calm, and collected in the process. In fact, they enjoy it. Others can't deal with any demanding situation and frequently find themselves upset.

Why the differences? Because the impact of stress depends on one's resiliency (or vulnerability) to stress. Your *stress resiliency* is a function of:

* Your physical condition (physical health, fitness, stamina)
* Your mental condition (mental health, emotional control)
* Your personality (how you typically look at, think about, and deal with the world)

For example, you know that when you are tired it is very difficult to deal with stressful events. And the same holds if your emotions are right on the surface, or if you always behave in a hostile way when things don't go right.

You can increase your resiliency to stress (another key to being in control) by increasing your physical and mental toughness and by becoming more aware of how your personality helps and hinders your ability to deal with problems. More about this in Part Three.

Apparent Causes vs. the Real Cause of Your Stress

Following are some common sources of stress. Put checkmarks beside the items that are creating stress for you.

Common Sources of Stress Checklist

Job-related sources of stress:
- [ ] Poor relationship with boss
- [ ] Workload too heavy or too light
- [ ] Time pressure, deadlines, rapid pace of the work
- [ ] Lack of direction (e.g., not clear what my role is, what's expected of me)
- [ ] Conflicts in expectations, values, ethics, personalities
- [ ] Uncertainty regarding company's future or my career
- [ ] Lack of feedback regarding my performance
- [ ] Lack of support
- [ ] Poor communication
- [ ] Lack sense of accomplishment, not making a meaningful contribution
- [ ] Downsizings, layoffs, reductions in force, firings

☐ Demands for higher productivity
☐ Inadequate work space or equipment
☐ Workaholic bosses, Type A bosses
☐ Meetings
☐ Distracting noise
☐ Poor personal performance
☐ Information overload
☐ New job responsibilities
☐ Budget cuts
☐ Commuting
☐ Poor quality of work done by others
☐ Increased competition
☐ Product recalls
☐ Government regulations
☐ Change
☐ Merger, acquisition, divestiture, reorganization
☐ Understaffing
☐ Politics, bureaucracy
☐ Incompetent and/or unmotivated people
☐ Rapid growth of business or decline in business
☐ Pressure for numbers, emphasis on quantity and/or speed

Family-related sources of stress:*

☐ Unsatisfying relationship with family member
☐ Difficulty communicating with family member
☐ Lack of time with family
☐ Health problems of family member
☐ Drug or alcohol addiction of family member
☐ Separation, divorce, remarriage, marital problems
☐ Social or school problems of family member
☐ Death of family member
☐ Change in residence
☐ Financial problems
☐ Challenges of parenthood

*Define family in whatever way is meaningful to you.

Personal sources of stress:

☐ Low self-esteem
☐ Negative thinking (pessimism, cynicism, hopeless-
ness, apathy)
☐ Low frustration tolerance
☐ Inability to deal with my emotions (emotional out-
bursts, uncontrolled temper, inability to express feel-
ings)
☐ Excessive competitiveness
☐ Being a perfectionist
☐ Health problems
☐ Drug or alcohol addiction
☐ Unclear personal values, long-range goals and plans
☐ Difficulty adjusting to major disappointments
☐ Difficulty asserting myself
☐ Difficulty getting through to other people
☐ Type A behavior, impatient, hostile, jumping from
one task to another
☐ Not in the right job for me
☐ Excessive behavior (overeating, drinking, working)
☐ Inadequate time-management skills
☐ Letting "little things" get to me

In the spaces below, write down exactly what is "causing"
the greatest stress in your job, family, and personal life:

Job-related:_____

_____

_____

_____

Family-related:_____

_____

_____

_____

Personal:_____

_____

_____

_____

Now I've got some good news and some bad news for you. First the bad news. Your stress can be caused directly by some event in your environment (e.g., extreme heat or cold, a loud noise, a physical injury). But, by far, most of your stress is self-induced. Self-induced stress is caused not by external events such as a traffic jam, a demanding boss, losing your job, or a pile of unfinished work but by the way you *look at* and *interpret* those events. There is nothing "out there" that is inherently stressful. A traffic jam is just a traffic jam and a pile of unfinished work is just a pile of unfinished work—until you look at these events as representing some sort of gap between what you want and what you have and interpret them as stressful events.

Stress is in the eye of the beholder, not in the event. It's an inside job. It's created between your ears—in your mind. The real cause of stress is how you look at and think about the event. The real cause of your stress is you! That's the bad news.

"People aren't disturbed by things, but by the views they take of them."

—Epictetus

And you don't even have to be looking at an actual event to perceive it as stressful. You can just be thinking about it. It might be a past event or something that *might* happen in the future. Just the thought of it will cause you to be distressed. This means that virtually anything real or imagined can cause you stress if you look at it or think about it as being stressful. Likewise, virtually nothing can cause you stress if you don't look at it as stressful. So it is very important to distinguish the *apparent* cause of your stress (your demanding boss, the traffic jam) from the *real* cause (how you look at and think about that situation). You can use this distinction to your great advantage as I will show you momentarily.

```
┌─────────────────────────────────────────────────────────┐
│               STRESS IS AN INSIDE JOB!                    │
│      IT'S CAUSED BY WHAT HAPPENS BETWEEN YOUR             │
│    EARS, BY HOW YOU LOOK AT, THINK ABOUT, AND            │
│                 RESPOND TO EVENTS.                        │
└─────────────────────────────────────────────────────────┘
```

The Automatic vs. the Conscious Nature of Your Response to Events

You don't go around purposely causing yourself stress. But over time you develop ways of looking at and reacting to various situations. You have been conditioned to look at some situations as stressful, some as crises, some as very frustrating, some as major disappointments. This labeling of events and your subsequent stress reactions have become automatic habits. You don't even realize what you are doing. You just automatically and unconsciously label and react. It only takes a millisecond. For example, you automatically see a traffic jam as a stressful event and unconsciously go immediately into your stress reaction.

And now for the good news. That stress is an inside job is also the good news because *you can control what goes on between your ears.* You don't have to automatically label events as stressful and go into a stress reaction. You can control how you look at, think about, and respond to events. Why? Because of your secret weapon: your power to make conscious choices and to take action that supports your choices.

You have the power to choose *how* you look at, think about, and respond to events, including events over which you have no control. This is really important. You always have a *choice.* When a potentially stressful problem occurs, you can consciously choose how you want to look at it, think about it, and deal with it. You don't have to automatically go into a stress reaction. You have options, healthier and more constructive options.

For example, you might choose to look at a company reorganization as a threat to your job security or as an exciting opportunity to develop new working relationships and skills. You might choose to be angry, to take it in stride, to roll with the punches, to fight, to flee, or to create something new. *It's your choice.*

It's all in how you look at it. And you can consciously choose how you want to look at it. This is especially good news because it is often much easier to change how you look at and think about events than it is to change the events themselves.

> STRESS MANAGEMENT IS AN INSIDE JOB!
> YOU CAN CONSCIOUSLY CHOOSE HOW YOU LOOK
> AT, THINK ABOUT, AND RESPOND TO EVENTS.

So, the key to being in control, cool, calm, and collected when dealing with potentially stressful events is to:

- Recognize the event as a gap between what you want and what you have.
- Recognize the situation as an opportunity to make a conscious choice about how you want to look at, think about, and respond to the gap.
- Make a conscious choice and take action that supports your choice.

This "making conscious choices and taking supporting action" approach to potentially stressful situations allows you to deal with the stress quickly and decisively, right at its source. You can then deal with problems in a cool, calm, collected, positive, productive, and healthy manner, thus greatly increasing your effectiveness in creating the results you desire most in your life.

Who's responsible for your stress—and for your effectiveness, health, and happiness? *You* are. You can't depend on others (including your employer) to take care of you. Although you can get valuable assistance from other people, managing your stress level is really a do-it-yourself project. You have to accept personal responsibility for taking good care of yourself. This is important. Is it clear to you that your experience of stress depends on how *you* look at a situation? And who controls how you look at a situation? You! So who controls how much stress you experience? You!

For instance, if a driver cuts you off on the highway and you automatically get all worked up and angry, remind yourself that the other driver did not make you angry. The event did not cause your anger, your stress. You (i.e., your unconscious, automatic response) caused your anger. You don't have to settle for that old response. You can choose a more effective, healthier response. Simply say something like "Where did that guy learn how to drive?" and let it go at that without getting yourself all worked up and seething with anger. It's your choice!

Although we love to blame someone or something outside ourselves for our problems and our stress, this book's approach places the responsibility for *your* feelings of stress where it belongs, in your hands and in your control!

You have the power to respond to any situation with positive, constructive thoughts and actions or to react with negative, nonproductive thoughts and actions. It's your choice.

Part Two

Your Very Own Command and Control Center

In Part Two, you start developing a practical, lifelong Personal Effectiveness Plan that will make you far more productive, healthier, and happier. It's a plan that you can use daily to create the life you truly desire.

The first step, Chapter 4, is to make sure you are serious about wanting to run your own life more effectively. The second step, Chapter 5, will help you clarify the life you truly want and the values you want to use to guide your approach to life. These steps result in your Command and Control Center, a frame of reference that will help you make wise choices every day and the first part of your Personal Effectiveness Plan.

4

Who Do You Want to Run Your Life?

You really can make a major difference in your life. But to do so, you need to make a *deep-down, fundamental choice* about who you want to run your life—you or someone (or something) else.

Being in charge of your own life means basing your behavior on your own conscious choices and accepting responsibility for the consequences of your behavior. It means not blaming circumstances or others for your actions or results. It means living your life from a proactive stance rather than a reactive one.

This is one of the most important choices you will ever make in your whole life. Forget your past. Today really *is* the first day of the rest of your life. Choose who (or what) you want to run your life from here on. You have the personal power to make this choice. What's it going to be?

☐ 1. I choose to run my own life! I choose to make conscious choices about the course of my life and to take actions that support my choices. I choose to be personally responsible for the consequences of my actions.

☐ 2. I choose not to run my own life! I choose not to make conscious choices about the course of my life. I choose not to be personally responsible for the consequences of my actions. Instead, I choose to have the following people or circumstances run my life:_____

I certainly hope you chose option 1. If so, say it again, this time with feeling: I *absolutely, positively* choose to run my own life. I choose to make conscious choices about the course of my life and to take actions that support my choices. I *am* personally responsible for the consequences of my actions.

Great! Now say the following out loud and with deep-down conviction that convinces *you* and everyone else in the universe: "Yes! I am totally committed to running my own life!" This may be a choice you want to make every morning for the rest of your life. Imagine the possibilities just doing that would create for your life!

Supporting Actions

Some actions that will support your choice to run your own life are as follows:

1. **Live your life with personal integrity.** Be true to yourself, to your most deeply held values. Act in a way that expresses who you really are. Be authentic. Do what you know is the right thing to do. Be honest with yourself. Say what you mean and mean what you say. Do what you say you are going to do—live by your word.

> *"To thine own self be true,*
> *and it must follow, as the night the day,*
> *Thou canst not then be false to any man."*
>
> —William Shakespeare, Hamlet

2. **Live your life with courage.** One major obstacle that can keep you from taking charge of your life is worrying about what other people think. There's always going to be someone who won't like what you do or say. It takes real courage to be true to yourself regardless of what others may think. Likewise, it takes courage to make your own choices—to dare to be different, if that's what's involved. It takes courage to do what you feel is truly right when that might run against the corpo-

rate culture, current practices, or norms of the people you are dealing with.

Many executives, managers, and professionals cling to a false sense of security for fear that things could get even worse. They don't make waves, they don't rock the boat, they don't speak up. They don't contribute their great ideas. Instead, they trade what could be a more exciting and satisfying life for a life of fear and dissatisfaction.

Courage is the ability to acknowledge fear and anxiety and to walk through it on the way to your goal. It's okay to be afraid. It's human. Fear can be a great help by making you more alert, more open to alternatives, more focused on effective action.

It takes courage to face life's big tests. It takes even more courage to face life's little tests—the little things that block our path to where we want to go or keep us from being whom we want to be. Be courageous. Have the courage to be yourself, regardless of which way the wind is blowing. Have the courage to change, to stay the same, or to bend when that's the right thing to do. And have the courage to take good care of yourself, to care about your life.

3. **Live your life with a commitment to action.** What is it that allows some people to overcome enormous obstacles to become successful, happy, and healthy while others give up and barely survive? Action. The people who are successful are not always the smartest, the fastest, the strongest, or the richest. The people who are successful are those who make conscious choices about what they truly want and take action—consistent, persistent action—to make it happen.

Commitment is unwavering determination to produce the results you say you are going to produce. Committed people rule out excuses. They just won't allow any barriers, any problems to keep them from following through. They kill off possible obstacles to their success (e.g., by leaving extra early to get to the city for a critical meeting, or by not bringing "fat food" into their home). They are convinced they can do whatever needs to be done, and they make the extra effort. They do their homework. They're well-prepared. They take action.

A person with a commitment to action doesn't "hope" to have a better relationship with the family and doesn't "try" to increase productivity or quality. He or she just does it. Commitment to taking action will conquer all the reasons and excuses why "it can't be done". Commitment to action transforms dreams into reality.

> *"Until one is committed, there is hesitancy, the chance to draw back, always ineffectiveness. . . . The moment one definitely commits oneself, then Providence moves too. All sorts of things occur to help one that would never otherwise have occurred. A whole stream of events issues from the decision, raising in one's favor all manner of unforeseen incidents and meetings and material assistance, which no man could have dreamed would have come his way. I have learned a deep respect for one of Goethe's couplets: 'Whatever you can do, or dream you can, begin it. Boldness has genius, power, and magic in it.' "*
>
> —W. H. Murray
> The Scottish Himalayan Expedition

How committed are you to taking action that will improve your personal effectiveness? Your health? The quality of your life? You can start exercising and strengthening your commitment-to-action muscle, if it's really out of shape, by making a commitment to do something small and doing it. For example, commit to greeting your spouse after work with a hug and kiss three days in a row—and then do it. Or commit to take the garbage or recyclables out on time—and do it. Or just make any promise and keep it. Live your commitments!

To check on whether you are actually living your commitments, periodically look at your actions. What do your actions say about your commitments? If you have no actions to match your commitments, then in reality you have no commitments.

```
COMMITMENT = ACTION
NO ACTION = NO COMMITMENT
```

4. **Live your life in control of yourself.** Stay in control of what you can control—your thoughts, your emotions, your actions. No more "they made me do it." No more "she made me so angry." No more "I'm just a poor, helpless victim."

Being in control of yourself facilitates getting the results you want. For example, if you are in control of yourself during mergers, downsizings, or restructurings, you can be an effective, productive, healthy, and happy employee (if those are results you desire).

Start acting like an empowered individual. Learn to replace the words "that's life and there's nothing I can do about it" with "that's life and there *is* something I can do about it." Be an "inner winner." Stay focused on creating the results you desire most in your job, family, and personal life and don't waste your time and energy on negative thoughts, emotions, and actions. Be a powerful person, truly in control of your thoughts, emotions, and actions and in charge of your life. Live your life proactively, in the create-your-own-life mode.

5. **Live your life consciously.** Wake up! Be alive and alert. Be aware of what's going on in your life, aware of what shape you are in. Be aware of what you truly want from your job, your family, and your personal life—of what you value most. Recognize what's working for you and what's not. Consciously choose to look at, think about, and deal with events in a way that will help you achieve what you want, not hinder you. Consciously choose to use your energy wisely in specific situations.

If your actions are not effective in producing the results you want, living consciously means asking someone else for help. When faced with a situation you don't know how to handle, one great choice you have is to ask for help. Listen, workaholics and extremely self-reliant types, John-Roger, coauthor of *Life 101*, said in an article in *Your Personal Best*: "I ask for help when I need it. I don't think there's anything great about being a martyr to get a job done. What's wrong with being smart enough to ask for help when you need it? If I'm doing my personal best and things still get beyond me, I ask for help. To me, that's being good to myself."

A Visible Sign

Go ahead. Make my day. As a sign that you are emotionally ready to do what is needed to live your life in a cool, calm, collected, positive, productive, and healthy manner, sign the following personal commitment to action:

I AM COMMITTED TO RUNNING MY OWN LIFE!

I dare to care about me! I care about the quality of my life, and about my capacity to be of service to others.

I choose to be in charge of my own life, to make a difference in my own life. I choose to live my life with personal integrity, courage, and a commitment to taking action that will create the results I truly desire in my job, family, and personal life.

I choose to be in control of what I can always control—my thoughts, emotions, actions. And I choose to live consciously, always alert to the results I want in my life, to what's working and not working, and to asking for help when I need it.

I am committed to learning and doing whatever is needed to live my life in a cool, calm, collected, positive, productive, and healthy manner!

_____

signature

I want to acknowledge the fact that you have read up to this point in the book. This accomplishment is evidence of your commitment to being a more effective, healthier, and happier you. You have already made the most difficult choice. You've chosen to take charge of your life, day in and day out.

You're emotionally ready to put together a Personal Effectiveness Plan that will empower you to create a really great life for yourself. Congratulations!

```
I CHOOSE TO
RUN MY OWN LIFE
WITH

• Personal integrity
• Courage
• Commitment to action
• Control of myself
• Awareness
```

The Life You Want and Your Guiding Values

You've got to have a dream to make a dream come true.

The whole purpose of having a Personal Effectiveness Plan is to make creating the life you want a lot easier and more enjoyable. After all, it's very hard to create the life you want if you aren't clear on what kind of life that is. This chapter helps you clarify what you want most from your job, your family, and your personal life, and what values you want to use to guide your approach to life. How will you know when you've hit upon what would be a great life for you? Listen to your conscience. Use your intuition. Feel your gut reactions. You will feel the pull. You will be excited and will want to get going on making it happen. A concise statement of the life you truly want and your guiding values will be summarized in what we'll call your *Command and Control Center.* Your Command and Control Center will affect virtually everything you do in your life. It is extremely important to make your statement as *clear* and *powerful* as possible, so that you can use the many choices you make each day to *help* you create that kind of life, rather than choices that *hinder* its creation.

When you know exactly what you want to do with your life and what kind of person you want to be, your whole approach to life is quite different. You are a person on a mission. You are a person with guiding values that are clear to you and clear to the people you interact with. You are powerful. You walk and talk differently. You act differently. You make things happen. This transformation allows you to approach life—and its problems and stress—in a cool, calm, collected manner!

A clear statement of what you want your life to be like results in a sharper sense of self-identity, more self-assurance, and greater decisiveness. People who haven't really thought about what their mission and guiding values are tend to drift through life, letting the winds of fate blow them around. Such people have trouble making wise choices, since they don't know what they want out of life or what is of value to them. They are often fearful, stressed, and strained, because they rarely take a value-based stand on anything, including themselves. They pay a high price for their lack of a clear vision of the kind of life they want and their lack of consciously chosen guiding values.

I will also share with you some enormously powerful secrets for making wiser choices and taking wiser actions all day long, so that you can produce the results you desire most in your job, family, and personal life with incredible velocity, efficiency, and joy—and with a lot less stress.

> *"If one advances confidently in the direction of his dreams, and endeavors to live a life which he has imagined, he will meet with success unexpected in common hours."*
>
> —*Henry David Thoreau,* Walden

The Life You Truly Want

First, develop a written statement describing the kind of life you truly want *and are willing to put forth the effort to create.* You will obviously want to give some thought to this. Read the helpful guidelines and the sample statement that follow, then put your thoughts down on paper and work on them for a while. When you are happy with what you've come up with, summarize the life you truly want in the space at the end of this section or on a separate sheet of paper.

Guidelines

1. You've got to have a dream to make a dream come true. This statement will include what you feel your primary mission

in life is. It will also include the roles and the results you want to create in your job, family, and personal life. Rank your roles in order of importance. The more your statement is in line with what you *really* want to do (e.g., desired roles such as spouse, parent, executive, civic leader, tennis player) and *really* want to accomplish or contribute in each role, the more power, excitement, and joy it will have for you. Try to be focused about your mission, roles, and desired results. Don't attempt to be everything, do everything, have everything. As Zig Ziglar, author of *See You at the Top* and motivational speaker par excellence, says, "I don't care how much power, brilliance, or energy you have, if you don't harness it and focus it on a specific target, you're never going to accomplish as much as your ability would allow."

2. Your statement can take your past history into account, but it doesn't have to be limited by it. Your past is past. You can do and be far more than you may think you can, so don't let past experience or current self-doubts limit your development of a statement that really moves you. Make sure your statement truly inspires and empowers you and reflects the real you.

3. Your statement doesn't have to be "perfect." Just sit down and start writing. Let it flow out of you. Get something down on paper, then work on it to come up with a statement you can start using right now. And consider it a "living" statement—something you will be looking at regularly and modifying as you desire.

4. If you have trouble developing your statement, try one or more of the optional clarification exercises at the end of this chapter.

Here is a sample statement:

The Life I Truly Want

My primary mission in life is to contribute significantly to the development of an effective and profitable company that produces a quality product, that truly cares about its customers and its own employees, that treats all people with respect and dignity, that is honest and ethical in all matters, and that is socially and environmentally responsible.

Other key aspects of my dream (the roles and results I want to create in my job, family, and personal life):

Desired roles (prioritized):	*Desired results:*
Healthy person	Enjoy lifelong wellness and all the energy I need to do what I want to do
Spouse	Enjoy a lifelong mutually supportive, loving relationship with my spouse
Parent	Enjoy developing competent, caring, self-expressive, responsible, and life-loving children
Executive	Rise to vice-president by making significant contributions to the company in areas of profitability, quality, and caring human resource management
Civic leader	Improve the quality of life in our community by exercising responsible leadership on the zoning board or school board, and by volunteering to assist annually with Special Olympics
Friend	Enjoy an active social life centered on my love of golf

This is just one example. Your own mission statement might be very short and nonjob-related. Likewise, your roles and desired results may be very different. It's quite okay if your mission turns out to be something like "my mission is to give love to every person I meet" or "my mission is to do my job well, stay healthy, be friendly, and enjoy life." Your mission does not have to be something grandiose, like saving the global environment or feeding everyone in the world.

When you are ready, use this space to summarize what you've come up with.

COMMAND AND CONTROL CENTER

The kind of life I truly want and am willing to put forth the effort to create is as follows.

My primary mission in life: _____

_____

_____

_____

Other key aspects of my dream (the roles and results I want to create in my job, family, and personal life):

Desired roles   *Desired results:*
(prioritized):

_____   _____

                           _____

                           _____

_____   _____

                           _____

                           _____

_____   _____

                           _____

                           _____

_____   _____

                           _____

                           _____

_____   _____

                           _____

                           _____

The Values You Want to Use to Guide Your Life

Now develop a list of the values you want to live by. This list is just as important as the statement you just prepared. It has to do with who you are as a person. Choose your values carefully and consciously. Your set of guiding values should be something you really treasure.

A guiding value is a strongly held value or principle that influences how you approach your life, including how you approach life's problems and stress. Guiding values provide you with guidance on how to approach your job, how to approach your family life, and how to approach your personal life.

Your guiding values reflect *the kind of person you want to be* across all the roles in your life—the kind of person you want to be known as. Your guiding values are the values you are committed to, the values you want to live by on a daily basis, the ones you are willing to take a stand for, and perhaps even are willing to die for.

Again, read the helpful guidelines that follow and the examples of guiding values that have stood the test of time. Then put your thoughts down on paper and work on them. When you are happy with what you've come up with, summarize your guiding values in the space at the end of this section.

Guidelines

1. Choose values that empower you. Your highest values should come from within and reflect who you really are, rather than from those values imposed upon you from the outside. Let your conscience be your guide.

2. Choose values that have stood the test of time. Enduring values will guide you through good times, tough times, and uncertain times. They will support you through unbelievable good fortune and through incredible pain and misfortune. This is particularly important in today's turbulent times when the complexity and rate of change in almost everything is mind-boggling and ethical guidelines are not always clear and not

always adhered to. (See *The Power of Ethical Management* in Recommended Resources at end of this chapter. This book is *must* reading.)

To survive and thrive under these conditions, you need a solid, unchanging core. Something stable and reliable that you can count on. A solid set of enduring values will provide that stable center from which you can approach change, problems, stress, and opportunities in a cool, calm, and confident manner.

3. Choose truth-based values. These are values that provide a solid foundation for building your life. For example, as Dr. Stephen Covey (author of *The Seven Habits of Highly Effective People*, which I recommend highly) notes, you may value material things or want lots of money, but the *enduring truth* is that orienting your whole life around the acquisition of material things or money is not a wise thing to do.

4. Include a value regarding the importance of taking good care of yourself. That is, your values should include not working so hard and being so dedicated to serving others that you do yourself in and are no longer able to enjoy life or contribute effectively.

5. Include as many or as few guiding values as you want.

6. Prioritize your top ten guiding values. This will clarify what is most important to you, what is next most important, and so on. This will make it a lot easier for you to make choices and take actions that help you be the kind of person you most want to be.

7. If you have trouble identifying or choosing your guiding values, the optional value-clarification exercises at the end of the chapter will prove helpful.

Here are some examples of guiding values and principles that have stood the test of time. This list should stimulate your thinking, not limit it. Look it over carefully, and consider choosing some of these values for your guiding values. Do not feel obligated or constrained by this list; your guiding values are your choice! They express the kind of person you are committed to *be*.

- Be 100 percent in charge of running my own life by making conscious choices with respect to how I live my life, and by being personally responsible for the consequences of my choices and actions.
- Be approaching my life from a proactive, create-my-own-life stance rather than a reactive, poor victim stance.
- Be aware that I always have choices in every situation, no matter how stressful, no matter how tough. Even if I can't do anything about the situation itself, I can always choose how I want to look at it, think about it, and deal with it.
- Be living my life with personal integrity and courage.
- Be in control of what I always can control—my thoughts, emotions, and actions.
- Be living consciously. Know what I want out of life, know what's working and what's not. Make timely adjustments. Get help when I need it.
- Be treating all people with respect and love. Be fair. Deal with people in a win-win manner. Be ethical.
- Be focused on making a difference in the lives of people rather than on accumulating things or being concerned only with serving myself.
- Be communicating and working with people in a positive, cooperative, low-stress manner.
- Be listening to others with a sincere desire to understand them, and then help them understand me.
- Be taking good care of myself (physically, emotionally, spiritually) so that I can feel good about myself, be productive, and be happy.
- Be living according to my carefully chosen priorities, putting first things first in my whole life and in my daily life.
- Be aware that I always reap what I sow—what I seed is what I get.
- Be cool, calm, and collected when dealing with problems and stressful situations.
- Be maintaining inner peace, living life in a peaceful, calm, relaxed state of mind.

- Be loving, compassionate, caring, giving, and forgiving.
- Be rejuvenating myself by playing, having fun, interacting with nature.
- Be making my day, and not relying on others to make my day for me.
- Be living in the present moment, rather than in the past or the future.
- Be bringing out the best in me and in others.
- Be mentally tough and focused. Be emotionally resilient.
- Be spiritually strong, vibrant, and joyful.

When you are ready, use this space to summarize your top ten guiding values:

1. _____

2. _____

3. _____

4. _____

5. _____

6. _____

7. _____

8. _____

9. _____

10. _____

Using Your Command and Control Center Every Day

You have now completed the work for your very own Command and Control Center: you have written your statement regarding the life you truly want and are willing to put forth the effort to create and have chosen your guiding values. This Command and Control Center is the first and most important part of your Personal Effectiveness Plan. (You'll assemble your complete Personal Effectiveness Plan in Chapter 14.) It is the dream that you are committed to making come true. Following are some guidelines on how to use your Command and Control Center every day to make wise choices and take wise actions.

What is a wise choice and a wise action? A wise choice or action *for you* is one that helps you create the life you truly want and helps you be the person you want to be (assuming that what you want is morally sound).

Guidelines

1. *Keep your Command and Control Center in front of you daily!* Review it and be fully aware of what you want in your job, family, and personal life and of the values you want to use to guide your life. This really empowers you. It pulls you to action. It makes you want to get out of bed in the morning. Once you have made a strong commitment to your personal mission and guiding values, you become alive!

When your desired results and your guiding values are in the forefront of your mind every day, they automatically direct, guide, and power your life. They give you a mindset for consistently making wise choices and taking wise actions, especially when multiple demands are clamoring for your immediate attention.

2. *Use your Command and Control Center to focus your life and energy on what you love.* Just as a magnifying glass harnesses and focuses the power of the sun, your Command and Control Center harnesses and focuses your energy on creating the life you love.

Let your Command and Control Center be an expression of love. Truly love your primary mission, your roles, and your values. Then the *doing* of your mission and the *being* of your values become a joy. Your journey through life becomes the joy, as does the achievement of your desired results.

3. *Use the hierarchy of roles, desired results, and values in your Command and Control Center to make wise choices.* Everything in your Command and Control Center is important to you, but the relative importance for any particular role or value may vary from time to time. It is this dynamic that guides your choices and actions. The guideline for making a wise choice

between options you value highly is straightforward—just choose the one you value *most*.

For example, say on Tuesday you have a lot of important work to catch up on at the office, your precious daughter is in a play at school, and you are exhausted. What's the wise choice? It depends on what has highest priority for you at the moment and what your guiding values are.

Or suppose being a successful professional, being a good parent, and being a healthy person are your top three priorities, in that order. If one day you have a heart attack, all of a sudden being a healthy person rockets to number one and that will dominate your choices and actions for some time.

Or say you've been offered a promotion. Is it wiser for you to take the promotion or to decline it? First, examine the pluses and minuses that come with accepting the promotion and those that come with declining the promotion. Then, if your Command and Control Center is in good shape, use it to sort through the issues (e.g., what will be the impact on what I want most in my job, family, and personal life? How does it fit with my guiding values?). If you are clear on what's *most* important to you at this time, you will be in a good position to make the wisest choice for you.

You can make difficult choices like these without agonizing over the choice and without feeling you had to go without something you valued because you can take pride and pleasure in having chosen the option *most* valued, as defined in your Command and Control Center.

4. *Use your Command and Control Center to balance your job, family, and personal life.* A quick glance at your Command and Control Center will help you remember (1) what you want most from your job or career; (2) what you want most from your family and/or social life; and (3) what you want most from your personal life. You can then schedule your time so it will produce the results you truly want most in these three areas of your life.

You Create Your Life by the Choices You Make

Every day you make many, many choices. You literally create your life by the choices you make, one choice at a time.

Sometimes you make big choices; for example, the line of work you choose to pursue, the jobs you choose to accept, the people you choose to associate with, the place you choose to live, how many hours you choose to work each day, how often you choose to have fun. And sometimes you make smaller choices; for example, what to wear, what to eat, when to buy gasoline, when to go to bed, when to speak up and when to keep quiet, or whether to exercise or not.

These points during your day when you have an opportunity to choose between two or more options I call *take charge points*. They are invitations to take charge of your life. Opportunities to be "in control." You can use each take charge point to create or support what you want most in your life. You can use them to make wise choices, to take wise actions. You can use them to fulfill your personal mission. To move your life in the direction you want it to go. To live your values. Whenever presented with a take charge point during your day, ask yourself which option would most help you create the life you truly want, and choose that option. Live consciously. Pay more attention to all the take charge points in your day. All the opportunities to *create the life you want—one choice at a time!* In fact, each moment presents you with an opportunity to empower yourself, to use your incredible power to choose the kind of person you want to be, the direction you want to go, the actions you want to take. You can *create* a take charge moment *right now*. Seize the moment!

> I CAN CREATE THE LIFE I TRULY WANT—
> ONE CHOICE AT A TIME!

"Decide now what you want from life and what you have to give in return. Decide where you are going and how you want to get there. Then make your start from where you stand at this very moment!"

—*Napoleon Hill*, Think and Grow Rich

Is it always easy to make wise choices when you have a clear personal mission and guiding values—a strong Command and Control Center? Of course not. Not always, but almost always! Life is messy and mysterious. We don't have all the answers. We don't have *total* control, but a well-thought-out Command and Control Center makes it a lot easier to make wise choices and will serve you well at all the take charge points in your life, especially when the going gets tough. To be in control of your life as much as possible, make sure that your Command and Control Center inspires you, that you are committed to it, and that you use it. This is essential. Choose to lead a life you value. A life based on *your* consciously chosen mission, roles, desired results, and values.

By making deliberate choices at the various take charge points during your day, you will naturally become more assertive and feel more in control of your life. Assertiveness and decisiveness inhibit anxiety! This allows you to enjoy the journey (the process of *living* your life) as well as your destinations (the results you create). Be in control of your life by making as many *wise* choices a day as possible. Become a master at using your take charge points powerfully and wisely. Use your Command and Control Center to stay focused on what's most important to you in life and stay the course! Be true to your values and passionate about your dream.

> I USE MY TAKE CHARGE POINTS AND MY
> COMMAND AND CONTROL CENTER TO MAKE
> WISE CHOICES AND TAKE WISE ACTIONS.

Recommended Resources

Blanchard, Kenneth, and Norman Vincent Peale. *The Power of Ethical Management.* New York: Ballantine Books, 1988.
Bolles, Richard. *What Color Is Your Parachute?* Berkeley, Calif.: Ten Speed Press, 1991. (Especially Appendix E on "How to Find Your Mission in Life.")

Covey, Stephen. *The Seven Habits of Highly Effective People.* New York: Fireside, 1989.

Miller, Emmett. *Power Vision: Life Mastery Through Mental Imagery.* Six audio cassettes plus workbook. Chicago: Nightingale-Conant, 1987.

Sinetar, Marsha. *Do What You Love, the Money Will Follow.* New York: Dell Publishing, 1987.

Optional Exercises

"All I want is a warm bed and a kind word and unlimited power."

—Ashleigh Brilliant

Following are three exercises that can help you clarify the kind of life you want and are willing to put forth the effort to create and what your guiding values are.

EXERCISE 1   Respond to these specific questions.

1. What do you truly want in your job or career? How much do you really want this? Why?
2. What do you truly want in your family and social life? How much do you really want this? Why?
3. What do you truly want in your personal life? How much do you really want this? Why?

Putting these headings on a piece of paper would help:

	I truly want	*Why*	*How much I want it*
In my job or career:	_____	_____	_____
In my family and social life:	_____	_____	_____
In my personal life:	_____	_____	_____

Use these questions to test the wisdom of your "truly wanted":
(1) Is it morally right? Is it for the highest good of all concerned?
(2) Will having this really make me happier, healthier, or more
effective? and (3) Can I emotionally commit myself to doing
what needs to be done to have it?

Make sure you know what you mean when you say "I
truly want. . . ." That is, if you say you truly want love or
health or success, what does love, or health, or success mean
to *you*? What has to happen for you to feel loved or healthy or
successful? Write that down, too.

Be as clear as you can about what you want. Your dreams
often involve images or mental pictures of the way you want
things to be—for example, a new house, a new job, a new
body. If possible, get an actual picture—a drawing or photograph—of what you want.

If what you want is something you've never had before,
find out or think through what it will be like to have it. If you
can't actually try a sample, imagine you already have it. What
does "it" look like? Smell like? Taste like? Feel like? Sound like?
Is this still what you really want?

And be sure to consider everything that comes with having
what you want—the positive and negative consequences of
having it. For example, if you really want that big promotion,
do you also want the additional hours away from home, the
greater responsibility, the more difficult problems? And how
does having the promotion affect other parts of your life (e.g.,
your family life, the quality of your relationships with people
you value, your health, your enjoyment of life). And what, in
turn, will these consequences lead to over the next few years?

Be sure you have a good fix on your current reality. Where
are you now relative to where you want to be? What's required
to get you from here to there? But don't let that current reality
limit what you want to be, do, or have. There are tons of real
stories in which ordinary people have achieved extraordinary
things.

Not clear yet on what you really want to do in life? Try this
delectable dozen questions.

   1. What do you really love doing? What makes you feel
      great? _____

2. What are you exceptionally good at? What are your special gifts? What's easy for you but hard for most other people?

_____

3. What's really important to you? What matters most to you? _____
4. What are you willing to take a stand for? _____
5. What are your strongest abilities, skills, and talents? _____
6. What really motivates you? What moves you to action? What do you feel passionate about? _____
7. What do you feel drawn to or feel in your bones that's you? Complete this sentence: I was born to _____
8. How do you spend your free time? Could this activity have something to do with what you really want to do with your life? _____
9. If you were absolutely certain that you would not fail, what would you do? _____
10. Complete this sentence: What I want to accomplish or contribute most is _____
11. What I *really* want to do is _____
12. Suppose you could have a one-on-one conversation with God right in your living room, and you could ask Him, "Why am I on this earth? What do you want me to do?" What do you think He would say? _____

EXERCISE 2   Go within yourself for the answers.

It is generally accepted that each of us has within us a personal mission, a purpose for being. A few of us are fortunate to have known since we were very young exactly what we wanted to do in life. But the rest of us must do a little exploring to discover our purpose. It is there, somewhere within us—we only have to discover it. One way to find it is to go deep within yourself and look for it. There are several ways to do this.

First, "begin with the end in mind," as Dr. Stephen Covey, author of *The Seven Habits of Highly Effective People*, says. He recommends that you visualize your own funeral and listen carefully to what four different speakers have to say about you. One speaker is from your family, one is from your work or profession, another is one of your friends, and the fourth is from your church or other community organization.

What would you like each of these speakers to say about you and your life? What kind of person were you? What contributions and accomplishments do you want them to cite? What difference have you made in their lives? What will they say was supremely important to you? Listen to the eulogy.

If you don't like what you hear, good. You're not dead yet; you can change the course of your life. Write your own eulogy. How do you *want* to be remembered? Write it down. What kind of life does the *real* you want to lead? What contributions do you want to make in your field, in your family, in your community, your society? What kind of person do you want to be known as? Do you want to be a world-class person as well as a world-class professional?

Dr. Covey, an expert in these matters, says that by doing this exercise what you value most will quickly become apparent. Your values will surface. And it's quite likely that when you seriously consider what matters most in your life, you'll discover that it has something to do with *love*: loving members of your family, reconciling bad relationships with people, expressing the love that's within you through your work—whatever your work might be.

Another way to go within is to use a professionally developed, guided imagery audiocassette program to enter a state of deep relaxation and be guided to the discovery of your personal mission and guiding values. This will calm your mind and provide direct access to your personal mission and your guiding values. I recommend an audiocassette program called *Power Vision: Life Mastery Through Mental Imagery,* by Emmett Miller, M.D. See the Recommended Resources at the end of the chapter.

EXERCISE 3   A systematic value-clarification exercise.

1. Read the list of 39 values on the following value-clarification form (Figure 2). At the bottom, add the values you chose from the list earlier in the chapter and others, if you wish.
2. In column 1, indicate the relative importance to you of each value, in terms of High (H), Medium (M), or Low (L).

Figure 2. Value-clarification form.

Personal Values	Importance High/Med/ Low/None	Rating Top 10
Achievement, accomplishment		
Advancement		
Adventure, excitement		
Ambition, working hard		
Challenging work		
Change, variety		
Cleanliness		
Closeness to God, salvation		
Competitiveness		
Cooperation, Teamwork		
Courage, standing up for your beliefs		
Creativity, imagination		
Economic security		
Effectiveness, competence		
Fame, being well known		
Family life		
Free time, leisure time		
Friendship, companionship		
Fun		
Health		
Helpfulness		
Honesty, sincerity, authenticity		
Independence, autonomy, freedom		
Inner peace		
Job security		
Leadership		
Love, affection		
Loyalty, dedication		
Logic, reason		
Orderliness		
Recognition from others		
Responsibility, accountability		
Participating with others, belonging		
Personal development		
Power, control, authority		
Self-respect		
Stability, minimal change		
Wealth		
Wisdom, learning, intellectual curiosity		

3. In column 2, give a rating of 1 to your most important value, a rating of 2 to your next most important value, and so forth until you've identified your top ten values.

4. In Figure 3, write your number one value in the box at the top and write in your other top values in the appropriate places. Do you see that your values are the sources of your motivation and satisfaction? If you know your values, then you know what motivates and satisfies you. Look at your top values and see if this seems to be the case for you. To what degree are your values currently being satisfied by your job, family, and personal life experiences? In terms of your values, what kind of career should you pursue? What jobs should you avoid?

Figure 3. What I value most.

```
              ┌─────────────────────┐
              │                     │
              │      #1 Value       │
              │                     │
      ┌───────┴───────┬─────────────┴───────┐
      │               │                     │
      │   #2 Value     │       #3 Value      │
      │               │                     │
┌─────┴───────────────┼─────────────────────┴─────┐
│                     │                           │
│      #4 Value        │        #5 Value           │
│                     │                           │
└─────────────────────┴───────────────────────────┘
```

\# 6 Value _____

\# 7 Value _____

\# 8 Value _____

\# 9 Value _____

\#10 Value _____

5. Sometimes our values are more obvious to other people than to ourselves. If you would like another reality check on your values, ask someone who knows you well to review the 39 values in Figure 2 and tell you which they believe are your five most important values and why they believe that.

Part Three

Choices That Will Definitely Help You Create the Life You Want in a Cool, Calm, and Collected Manner

Fasten your seatbelt. Get ready to feel spectacularly empowered. This is where it all gets real exciting! In this part of the book, you develop a lifelong strategy and the specific techniques for approaching problems, dealing with stress, and producing desired results in a consistently cool, calm, collected, positive, productive, and healthy manner. These personal effectiveness skills will dramatically enhance the effectiveness, health, happiness, and the overall quality of your life *every day*.

The Seven Daily Power Choices are presented in Chapters 6 through 12. They have proven to be very effective for hardworking executives, managers, and professionals. The seven choices are *unbelievably powerful* and will be key elements in your Personal Effectiveness Plan. (When you draft your Personal Effectiveness Plan in Chapter 14, you do not have to include all the supporting actions that are suggested for each of the Daily Power Choices. You will simply select the supporting actions that you truly want to use to make yourself more effective, healthier, and happier.) In Chapter 13 you make some fun choices that will really help you balance and enjoy your life.

6

Choose to Approach Problems in a Cool, Calm, Collected Manner

"Relax. I can handle this in a calm, effective manner."

The main idea behind Daily Power Choice 1 is to use normally stressful events to instantly trigger a more relaxed, more effective, in-control response, instead of your usual automatic, out-of-control stress response.

Once you get the hang of this, you'll find it really fun to use. You almost go around looking for stressful situations and problems so that you can show off your new cool, calm, collected, "relax, I can handle this" approach.

How It Works

By *instantly* replacing your automatic stress response with a cool, calm, collected response, you are able to deal with the problem situation and the people involved in a low-stress, humane way. You take positive, constructive steps to produce the result you desire instead of reacting emotionally and making things worse. You end up far more effective and a lot healthier. You improve your relationships with people, enhance your mental toughness and emotional control, and enjoy that *"I am* in control" feeling!

When do you use Daily Power Choice 1? As soon as you realize you are in a potentially stressful situation, and you feel yourself starting to go into your automatic stress reaction. But . . .

It's Your Choice

Make a deep-down choice right now about how you are going to approach problem situations from here on:

☐ 1. I choose to approach problems instantly in a cool, calm, collected, in-control manner.
☐ 2. I choose to approach problems instantly in a hot-headed, stressful, fearful, out-of-control manner.

Wise Supporting Actions

I certainly hope you chose the first approach. Here are some specific actions that will allow you to instantly approach whatever problems come your way in a cool, calm, collected manner.

Instantly Take a Deep Breath and Make a Confident, Positive Statement

As soon as you realize you are starting to react to a problem situation with your automatic stress response, take a deep, cleansing breath (inhale slowly and deeply through your nose, expanding your abdomen and working your way up to the top of your lungs, hold for a few seconds, then exhale slowly through your mouth or nose) and say something positive like, "Relax. I can handle this in a calm, effective manner." Consciously choose to use your energy wisely and effectively in this situation.

For example, you receive your monthly bank statement. It shows your savings account is $10,000 short of what it should be. You need to call the bank and tell them they've made an error. You are angry at their incompetence and ready to lay into them. But instead of doing that, you take a deep, cleansing breath and say to yourself: "Relax. I can handle this situation in a calm, effective manner." Then you pick up the phone and call to explain the problem.

This technique is incredibly simple, but incredibly powerful. It works! Use it!

Instantly Put the Situation in Perspective and Take It in Stride

Another way to approach a potentially stressful situation is to put it in perspective and take it in stride. Just let go of your anxiety and don't let it bug you any longer. Resume a positive attitude and move on. You can do this by using phrases like, "It's only a. . . ." or "How fortunate that. . . ." Here are some others:

"Oh well, nobody's perfect."
"It's not that important anyway."
"Slow down, take it easy, it's not worth dying for."
"Actually, the worst thing that can happen is . . . and I can handle that."
"This, too, shall pass."
"Relax, everything will work out fine."
"Oh well, I can't know everything."

For example, say to yourself:

"It's only a national sales meeting. Take it easy. It's not worth dying for."
"How fortunate that no one was killed or seriously injured in the accident."
"Oh well, nobody's perfect" (as you accidently delete all the information you put in the computer today), or, "I may not be perfect, but parts of me are excellent!" (As Ashleigh Brilliant would say.)
"I didn't get to finish painting the guest room and our guests are coming tomorrow. Oh well, it's not that important anyway. It will just be wonderful to see Howard and Angela again and have a chance to relive old memories with them."
"Actually, the worst thing that can happen is I'll miss the

plane and have to reschedule the meeting, and I can handle that."

Instantly Defuse the Situation with Humor

Laugh at yourself or at your predicament; jest for the health of it. Use positive humor, and avoid sarcasm or cynicism. Choose to play "gee ain't it funny" instead of "gee ain't it awful."

Instantly Suspend Your Judgment and Seek First to Understand—Diagnose Before You Prescribe

Human beings have a natural tendency to instantly judge events, people, statements, actions, or anything. This is especially true in stressful situations charged with strong feelings and emotions. This natural tendency is a major barrier to effective communication and effective action.

To dramatically improve your effectiveness, cultivate the ability to instantly suspend your judgment when presented with information that doesn't fit your point of view or values. Back off immediately and take a detached, nonjudgmental stance. Diagnose the situation before you prescribe a remedy (prescription without diagnosis is malpractice).

Be willing to listen and gather more information in a relaxed state. Learn what the other point of view is all about and what merits it may have. Back away far enough so you can see the bigger picture—perhaps even see how a variety of viewpoints fits the overall panorama.

It helps to assume right up front that the other person's point of view *does* have merit, that it is worthwhile. Keep in mind that the way *you* see things *is* the way you see things. And the way other people see things *is* the way *they* see things. Acknowledge that this is true for each individual, including that other person you are dealing with who "can't possibly see it that way."

This ability to back away and take a nonjudgmental stance can greatly reduce your stress, help you adjust your approach to people with different values and experiences, and significantly improve your relationships and increase your effectiveness with them.

So, rather than jumping to conclusions, suspend your judgment for a minute. Listen carefully and observe the feelings of the other person. Hear the other person out (note: teenagers' number-one complaint is that their parents don't listen to them). Gather some facts about the situation, then involve the other person in problem solving as you continue conversing in a cool, calm, respectful manner.

Real communication occurs when you purposefully seek to truly understand the other person and avoid your tendency to instantly evaluate or disapprove. Make a sincere effort to see the situation from the other person's point of view, to discover what is assumed, to sense how it feels, to see the matter from the other person's mindset.

Test yourself. Next time you get into a potential argument, avoid making an instant judgment. Try first to repeat the individual's statement and describe his or her feelings accurately. You'll find that the stress and the defensiveness—yours and the other person's—disappear fast when your only intent is to understand, not to judge. *Instantly* suspend your judgment and seek first to understand. Do it. It works beautifully!

Instantly Protect Yourself From the Negative Influence of Other People

I first heard this great idea from Ed Foreman, developer of *The Successful Life Program*. Negative people can trigger your automatic stress response very easily—if you let them. To prevent this, as soon as you see them coming, mentally zip yourself into a protective positive cocoon and don't let their negativity penetrate. Radiate your positive attitude and greet them with a positive statement.

Avoid asking negative people how they are. If they bombard you with negative statements, respond instantly with a positive statement. Eventually, they may get the message that you aren't interested in the "let's be negative" game. If not, just tell them so. What's more, don't let negative, disrespectful people in your organization get you down. Treat yourself with respect and dignity regardless of how they treat you.

Don't Sweat the Small Stuff

Increase your tolerance level for problems. Learn to allow some problems to exist without distressing you.
Remember the equation in Chapter 3?

(Want − have) × (importance to you) = stress potential

This indicates that one way to reduce or even eliminate your stress is to instantly reduce the importance you give potentially stressful events. If a potentially stressful situation erupts, quickly ask yourself, "How important is this to me?" Is it big stuff or is it small? Is it worth getting all worked up over? Is it worth my energy? Can I make a difference?

If it's really important, declare it so. Take action and expend the energy required to deal with the situation. But if it's not important, say so. Conserve your energy, ignore it, let it be, and move on to something more worthy of your energy.

For example, suppose you overhear your children arguing outside. Instead of getting all worked up and running outside to break it up (and getting yourself entangled in the argument), just take a deep, cleansing breath, make a big smile, and say to yourself, "Relax. I'm leaving my mind and body out of this one."

Since you don't have enough time and energy to solve all the problems in life, choose your battles carefully. You can also look at it as learning to live with some of the gaps in your life. Just because you experience a gap between what you want (a clean house) and what you have (a messy house), it doesn't mean you have to get physically and mentally distressed over it. You can choose to ignore it, accept it, or work on closing the gap in a relaxed, effective way.

Tom Crum, a martial arts expert, says in his book *The Magic of Conflict*, "The best rules I've ever heard for handling stress are these:

1. Don't sweat the small stuff.
2. It's all small stuff.
3. Since it usually doesn't work to fight, and it doesn't work to flee, *flow!"*

By *flow*, Crum means take it in stride—work with or "dance" with the other forces operating in your environment, rather than against them.

I'm not sure all the stuff we encounter in our lives in small. But it's clear that people do allow themselves to get very distressed over a lot of small stuff. This is why it's so important to be clear on what's most important in your life (as you determined in Chapter 5). Your Command and Control Center helps you decide what is small stuff and what is not.

Instantly Relabel the Situation in a Way That Empowers You

Whenever you run into a gap between what you have and what you want, you automatically label it as a problem, a stressful situation, or a crisis. Instead, choose a label that empowers you rather than drains you.

How you label a gap in your life has tremendous impact on how you look at it and deal with it. Instead of calling it a problem, call it a challenge or an opportunity to show your personal best. Instead of labeling it a miserable failure, label it a great learning experience. Instead of calling it stressful, call it exciting. And instead of labeling yourself as weak in one area, see yourself as strong in lots of other areas.

When in Doubt, Breathe Deeply!

Your body and brain need oxygen to operate effectively. *It is essential.* (Did you ever notice how long people live after they stop breathing?) Stress usually makes you breathe rapid and shallow breaths, thus diminishing the supply of oxygen to your body, especially to the brain.

As soon as you find yourself in a stressful situation, and you notice your breathing becoming tense, short, and shallow, breathe in the opposite manner, with slow, deep breaths. You'll instantly feel more clear-headed, more relaxed, and more in control. That's why slow, deep breathing is an important part of nearly all stress-control techniques.

Use your breath to manage your physical and emotional reactions to stress. Mastering this skill will allow you to remain cool, calm, and collected in *any* pressure situation!

Develop a Cool, Calm, Collected Manner

A manager called me recently and said she really knew this instant relaxation technique took hold when her two-year-old son spilled grape juice on their new carpet. She instantly chose to relax and stay in control. She calmly chose to look at that potentially stressful situation as "my child spilled grape juice on the carpet" (what happened, happened), and she chose to clean it up without getting angry, without screaming and yelling, and without demeaning her son.

Make it a game. Turn stressful situations into cues for an instant relaxation response. What situations can you think of right now whereby you might experiment with this very powerful technique?

> I CHOOSE TO APPROACH PROBLEMS IN A COOL,
> CALM, COLLECTED MANNER EVERY DAY.

```
  ........
  :      :
  :  7   :
  :      :
  ........
```

Choose to Rest, Relax, and Rejuvenate Your Body

Give your body a break.

If you churn inside when you get upset or worried (especially if you tend to hold it all in), if your muscles tighten up when you are under stress, if you get angry and your "blood boils" when things go wrong, if you are chronically fatigued or burned out—then choose to rest, relax, and rejuvenate your body every day. This is Daily Power Choice 2.

How It Works

Simply giving your body a chance to rest and recover from the strain it's subjected to is one of the most effective ways to manage and counteract the effects of stress. It gives your body a chance to recuperate and return to a relatively stable state.

Taking "body breaks" as needed every day helps break that constant state of tension you can get yourself into each day. If the buildup of stress goes unchecked, it will accumulate until, one day, it gets to be too much. Then your body will give you a signal you can't miss—a heart attack, gastrointestinal problems, painful arthritis, or a stroke. Remember, if you don't do something with that energy, it will definitely do something to you.

Body breaks allow you to get optimal performance out of yourself through pacing. You can actually speed up and be more productive by occasionally taking body breaks during the day to rest so your body can release pent-up stress, recuperate, and recharge. Timing is key. Your body will tell you when it needs a break. Listen to your body's signals. As soon as you feel your muscles tightening, your stomach churning, your head aching, your "blood boiling," take action. Don't wait until you get home or until all the work is done or until your vacation comes along. If you learn to rest, relax, and rejuvenate your body during each day, you will improve your personal effectiveness and productivity, preserve your health, maintain your energy level throughout the day, and not come home from work exhausted.

It's Your Choice

Make a deep-down choice right now about how you will deal with the physical tension and strain that builds up in your body over the course of your day.

☐ 1. I choose to take body breaks during the day to release the stress energy that builds up within me and creates physical tension and strain. I won't wait; I won't hold it in. I'll get it out of my system and give my body a little time to rest and rejuvenate itself so that I don't damage my body or ruin my health.

☐ 2. I choose not to take body breaks during the day. I'll just ignore the buildup of tension and physical strain in my body. I'll try to hold it in, tough it out. So what if I do run myself ragged every day? Maybe I'll deal with the pain by drowning it in alcohol or numbing it with drugs. I might have a doctor take a look at that ulcer that's killing me—just as soon as I get back from. . . . But I'm not going to mention the pain and weird sensations I've been feeling in my chest lately. I'm sure I don't have any heart problems. I don't have time for that.

Wise Supporting Actions

I hope you chose the first option. Here are some specific actions that will allow your body to rest, relax, and rejuvenate so that you can be more effective, healthier, and happier.

Let Off Steam. Release the Tension. Talk It Out.

When you feel that buildup of stress start churning inside your body and you just don't know what to do, give your body a break. Get it out of your system right away. This is especially important for you quiet, reserved types. Don't hold it in. Don't sit there and stew. Get that energy out immediately, in a way that does not harm anyone or anything, of course. Pound on something nonbreakable and preferably soft (a pile of magazines, a chair cushion) or take a newspaper, roll it up, and pound it on a table or desk to get that energy out. Scream or recite your favorite stress-relieving words—out loud or silently—but with all the relevant gestures. Or talk to someone who is supportive. Tell the person what's bothering you and how you feel about it. If they're not present, call them on the phone. If no one is readily available, talk to yourself—say, ". . . is bothering me and I feel. . . ." Verbalizing your feelings brings out that pent-up energy and is therapeutic.

Pace Yourself. Take Body Breaks During the Day.

It helps to plan your pace for the day. Learn to predict the amount of work you can realistically accomplish in a given time, and then consciously pace yourself to fit that schedule, incorporating body breaks as needed.

How often have you continued working when your body was straining for a break? Pay attention to your body's needs and rhythms. Whenever you fight yourself physically, you are not doing yourself a favor. Take a body break when your body signals the need for it. Let it recharge.

As soon as you feel signs of physical stress and strain, get up, take a walk, get a drink of water, have a friendly conversation with someone, sit in a comfortable chair, or get some fresh air. Do anything that will allow you to break that constant buildup of stress and strain, even if it is just for a minute or two.

If you are desk-bound, lean back in your chair, close your eyes, and take a couple slow, deep breaths. That will allow your body to recuperate a little and revitalize you for the next piece of work. Try it. It works great. You can just feel your body rejuvenating itself.

What's important is to do these things *as soon as* you feel the physical stress and strain setting in. Don't wait until lunchtime. Don't wait until you get home. Do it now!

Stretch Those Tense Muscles

As soon as you feel your back, shoulder, or neck muscles tightening up, take a minute to stretch those muscles. Using slow, easy movements, do some neck rolls and shoulder shrugs, or stretch your arms toward the sky. The key to minimizing the tension in your muscles is to stretch them as soon as you feel the tension. Don't wait for them to go into spasm.

Get a Good, Deep Restful Sleep at Night

"I have to get more sleep." How many times have you said that to yourself? Sleep is a biological necessity. Your body needs time to repair, recuperate, and reenergize. This is what sleep provides.

The December 17, 1990, issue of *Time* magazine had as its cover story the sleep deprivation crisis in the United States. It reported that choosing to forgo rest is a foolish and often perilous bargain. Millions of people who don't get enough sleep can't think, can't make appropriate judgments, and can't maintain long attention spans. They don't have much energy. Do you know of any jobs that require people to think, to make critical judgments, to maintain long attention spans, to have lots of energy? How about your job? With relentless "do more with less staff" campaigns the standard operating procedure of the day, we have corporations with layoff survivors who now work twelve, fifteen, or eighteen hours a day. People trying their hardest, but in reality, physically unable to give their best because they lack adequate sleep. (By the way, this is becoming a serious problem in Japan.)

Like any machine, the human body has its limits. Not getting enough good sleep is a major contributor to burnout (physical and mental exhaustion). Chronic lack of sleep can have serious adverse effects on learning, performance, relationships, communication, health and liveliness, basic civility, and compassion. Without sufficient sleep, people are irritable—tempers flare fast and out-of-control behavior is common.

The *Time* article suggested that most Americans no longer know what it feels like to be fully alert. They go through the day in a twilight zone. It's important to recognize when you aren't getting enough sleep. If you have trouble getting out of bed in the morning, and show up for work each day dead tired, only manage to get through the day by drinking lots of coffee, tea, or caffeine-rich soda, then consider the possibility that you are not getting enough sleep and not doing your body any favor. With each dose of caffeine you are beating a dead horse. The coffee might give your body a jolt to go another 100 yards, but soon you'll be exhausted again. Wake up! Get more sleep.

Not all sleeplessness is by choice. Some individuals suffer from genuine sleep disorders. But for most of us it is a choice—to get more sleep or to work late or stay up watching TV or whatever. In any case, the fact is that lack of sleep increases stress and performance problems, while rejuvenating sleep decreases those problems. Getting good sleep may be a wise and powerful choice for you.

Experiment. Try going to bed one hour earlier. If it helps, use an alarm clock to remind you when to *go* to bed. Cut back on the amount of caffeine you gulp down each day; instead, when you feel tired, take a five-minute rest and rejuvenation break. If possible, close your eyes and just let your body recover. You can feel it happening!

If you think you may have a chronic sleep disorder, schedule an appointment with a clinic that specializes in sleep disorders. (Pick up the phone and do it right now.) If you have only occasional trouble getting to sleep or staying asleep, and you have tried the obvious things, consider using an audiotape designed to help you get to sleep and stay asleep. Check your bookstore. I recommend one by Dr. Emmett Miller titled *Easing Into Sleep* (see Recommended Resources at the end of this chapter).

If you are approaching the burnout phase and are near

physical exhaustion, you may benefit significantly by taking the time to sleep longer and to take naps. Your body has a *lot* of recovering to do. Give it time to do it. Minimize nonessential activities for a while.

Use the Relaxation Response to Deeply Relax Your Entire Body Daily

You can systematically relax your entire body and let go of all the stress, strain, and tension that accumulates every day. Herbert Benson, professor of medicine at Harvard Medical School and author of *Beyond the Relaxation Response* (see Recommended Resources), found that a Relaxation Response can easily be elicited in people.

The *stress response* is characterized by increased blood pressure, heart rate, breathing, and body metabolism, and decreased flow of blood to the hands and feet. The *Relaxation Response* is physiologically the opposite: decreased blood pressure, heart rate, breathing rate, and metabolic rate, and increased flow of blood to the hands and feet. The subjective feelings include a sense of profound calm and clarity, and a feeling of being very relaxed, of pleasure, refreshment, well-being.

The Relaxation Response can be elicited by these simple steps:

1. Sit quietly in a comfortable position and gently close your eyes.
2. Let go of as much physical tension as you can. Start with your feet and progress upward, relaxing each muscle group as you go.
3. Tell yourself that "it's okay to relax my mind and body."
4. Breathe slowly and naturally. Focus on your breathing. As you exhale, say a special word silently to yourself or see it in your mind's eye. Your special word can be any word or phrase or spiritual affirmation that you find relaxing and comforting. Dr. Benson highly recommends the word or phrase reflect your personal spiri-

tual beliefs (e.g., "The Lord is my shepherd" or "Shalom") for maximum effect.
5. Continue for ten or twenty minutes.
6. Maintain a passive, relaxed attitude. This is very important. When distracting thoughts occur, say to yourself, "Oh well," and return your focus to repeating your special word on each exhalation.
7. Every now and then you can tell yourself, "It's okay now to r-e-l-a-x e-v-e-n m-o-r-e. I'm going to an even d-e-e-p-e-r level of total relaxation."

Practice this technique once or twice daily, but not within two hours after any meal. The method works best on an empty stomach, so that it doesn't have to compete physiologically with the digestion process. Soon you will be able to achieve a deep state of relaxation easily and very quickly. You will even be able to get into a relaxed state on command simply by taking a deep breath and saying your focus word or phrase as you exhale.

This daily deep relaxation is an excellent habit to develop. It breaks that dangerous constant buildup of stress every day and, in fact, has the opposite effect of stress. Deep relaxation feels like a deeply centered sense of peace, calmness, clarity, and control—a feeling that literally overflows into your life and makes all your challenges a lot easier and more enjoyable. And it prepares your mind and body for optimal performance. Your investment of ten to twenty minutes a day (or at least two or three times a week) in deep relaxation will generate a huge return on investment! You will become a more in-control person—less reactive, less open to provocation, and more tolerant of situations that would have frustrated or angered you in the past. You'll be more able to adapt and deal with events as they unfold.

Living your day in an alert, mentally relaxed state is what allows you to be cool, calm, collected, positive, productive, and healthy—regardless of what comes your way. Without a doubt, one of the finest ways you can treat yourself right is to choose to quiet your body and mind and enjoy ten to twenty minutes of deep relaxation every day!

An excellent tape that will help you achieve a deep state of relaxation is *Letting Go of Stress* by Dr. Emmett Miller (see Recommended Resources).

The Relaxation Response has also been used successfully to help treat specific health problems, such as headaches, back pain, chest pain (angina pectoris), high blood pressure, cancer, and insomnia. You can also use a slight variation of this method during rhythmic repetitive exercise to achieve the overall benefits of the Relaxation Response.

Recommended Resources

Benson, Herbert. *Beyond the Relaxation Response.* New York: Times Books, 1984.
Miller, Emmett. *Letting Go of Stress.* Audiocassette. Stanford, Calif.: Source Cassette Learning Systems, 1980.
———. *Easing Into Sleep.* Audiocassette. Stanford, Calif.: Source Cassette Learning Systems, 1981.

I CHOOSE TO REST, RELAX, AND REJUVENATE MY BODY AS NEEDED EVERY DAY.

Choose to Calm Your Mind, Be Centered, and Think Clearly Under Pressure

Calm your mind, and inner control and power you'll find.

Is your head is spinning, you can't concentrate, you can't think straight, you feel overwhelmed and out of control? Are you fearful or really worried about something? If you want a clear mind to help you produce the results you want, then choose to calm your mind, be centered, and think clearly every day. This is Daily Power Choice 3.

How It Works

Most of us spend our time doing one thing while thinking of something else. We are not completely focused on the present moment. We have mental chatter and various streams of thought going on in our heads all the time. What conversations are going on in your mind right now? How much of your attention is focused on this book? Is your mind somewhere else?

If your mind wanders uncontrollably, dwelling on distracting and distressing thoughts of what's happened in the past, what might happen, what should happen, you are not focusing your powers on the task at hand. You are trying to do one thing while your mind is off doing something else.

These distracting, stress-producing thoughts (fears, worries, negative thinking) make it difficult—if not impossible—to concentrate and lead to distorted thinking, poor decision making, and poor performance.

This Daily Power Choice helps you clear your mind of stress-producing thoughts, quiets the distracting conversations, and allows you to regain control of your mind. Whenever you focus *only* on the present, you relax! Your mind settles down, clears up.

This Daily Power Choice gives you another, more comprehensive view of reality that makes you feel more comfortable with yourself and with everything else and more effective and joyful in dealing with the world. It makes you more efficient by helping you deal in a focused manner with one thing at a time. So this power choice involves three basic ideas:

1. Clearing your mind of distracting, stress-producing thoughts
2. Bringing your mind totally into the present moment
3. Refocusing your mind on something peaceful and empowering

When do you use Daily Power Choice 3? As soon as you start having difficulty concentrating, can't think clearly, feel mentally in a rut, overwhelmed, or just can't get a worry or fear out of your mind; or when you are jumping from one task to another, or majoring in minors by doing lots of low-priority items but not getting to what's most important now. Even better, start each day by calming and centering yourself and carry that cool, calm, in-control feeling with you throughout the day. You'll enjoy a clear-headed, relaxed composure that allows you to focus, think clearly and creatively, and thus be more effective, more productive, and healthier.

It's Your Choice

Make a deep-down choice right now about how you want to deal with the mental stress and strain that makes it so difficult to focus your attention on the present task, to think clearly, and to perform well, especially when you are under pressure.

☐ 1. I choose to clear my mind of distracting, stress-producing thoughts, to bring it totally into the present moment, and to focus it on something peaceful and empowering, so that I can concentrate on what needs to be done, think clearly, be creative, make quality decisions, and greatly enhance my personal effectiveness, especially in pressure situations.

☐ 2. I choose to dwell on distracting, stress-producing thoughts of the past or future and let them disrupt my mental processes such that I can't concentrate, I can't think straight, I make rash decisions or no decisions, and I render myself ineffective or even counterproductive, especially in pressure situations.

Wise Supporting Actions

Please tell me that your mind was clear enough to choose option 1. Here are some specific actions that will allow you to use Daily Power Choice 3 so that you can be cool, calm, collected, positive, productive, and healthy, especially under pressure.

Take Brain Breaks During the Day to Clear, Calm, and Refresh Your Mind

Research indicates that people are far more productive if they take stress-relieving breaks during the day. They actually speed up and improve the quality of their work by taking time to slow down. And by changing their mental focus, they get out of their mental rut and free up their creativity.

One way you can regain control of your mind is to just stop and give your brain a break.

As soon as you feel mentally in a rut, can't think straight, or can't concentrate, stop what you're doing and take a brain break. Get up, take a walk, get a drink of water, have a friendly conversation with someone, go sit in a comfortable chair, read something of interest, get some fresh air, escape to a place of peace and quiet. Engage in an activity totally different from the one you were doing, an activity that brings your mind totally into the present and focused on something pleasant and relaxing. This interrupts that dangerous buildup of mental stress, relieves the strain on your brain, and refreshes your mental capabilities.

If you are desk-bound, simply lean back in your chair, close your eyes, take a few slow, deep breaths, and focus totally on your inhaling and exhaling. This will allow your mind to calm down, clear, recuperate, and revitalize you for the next piece of work.

Do these things as soon as you feel the mental stress and strain setting in. Don't wait until lunchtime. Don't wait until you get home. Don't wait for the weekend.

Focus Your Mind on Something Specific, Pleasant, and Calming

Take a minute to relax. Shake the physical tension out of your body. Then, for three minutes or longer, focus your mind *totally* on something specific, pleasant, and calming. It can be anything—a picture, an object, a peaceful word, a calming phrase, a spiritual affirmation, or a pleasant experience. Your mind will clear and become open, receptive, creative, and fully operational. Take slow, deep breaths as you do this.

This works because as complex as the mind is, it can only concentrate on one thing at a time. If you focus on a negative, stress-producing thought, your mind and body will respond stressfully. If you concentrate on something pleasant, your mind and body respond pleasantly—the Relaxation Response takes over.

Go through your photo albums or magazines and find a picture that readily produces a peaceful, easy feeling in you. Place the picture strategically on your desk (or wherever) and use it to calm your mind instantly. You can also get a picture in your mind of the most cool, calm, and collected person you know and focus on that image. This might be a business person, a professional athlete, or anyone else you admire for this characteristic.

Or revitalize your mind by taking a few minutes to mentally picture and relive a pleasant experience—a really relaxing time, a favorite vacation, the first warm day of spring, or whatever. You can create your own "movies in your mind" or use professionally developed "guided imagery" experiences available on audio and videocassettes (see Recommended Resources at the end of the chapter).

To create your own mental movie, recall the pleasant experience you want to mentally relive. Before you run the movie, describe the scene in detail: the setting, the context, what you are doing, your emotional state, what you see and hear, what the colors, smell, and feel of the place are like. Then run the movie. Experience fully this pleasant experience as if it were really happening right now. Smile. And when the movie is over and you are rejuvenated, return to your real world, ready to deal with it with renewed calm, clarity, and creativity.

Another excellent option is to use the Relaxation Response procedure presented in Chapter 7 to focus and clear your mind and reap the many physical and mental benefits.

I want to strongly encourage you to explore further what's available to you through meditation. Meditating is simply the process of calming and clearing your mind and refocusing it on one specific thing, activity, or idea with full awareness in the present moment. It is the art of keeping your mind focused on the task at hand in a cool, calm, and collected manner and dealing gently but effectively with any distracting thoughts that inevitably occur. Meditation exercises are neat ways to gain control over your thoughts and your mind (and your life).

In the Recommended Resources at the end of this chapter, I refer you to an excellent book by David Harp that contains a very clear, practical, and brief explanation of what meditation is. It also provides 30 three-minute meditations you can use to calm and refocus your mind anywhere anytime. This book is user-friendly and written in a good-humored way. Just reading it will make you feel cool, calm, and collected. It also shows you how to use the three-minute meditations to deal with thoughts of anger, self-judgment, fear, loss, loneliness, and emptiness.

I also recommend you take a look at the book by Lawrence LeShan. It's informative with respect to what people get out of meditation that makes them want to meditate daily, how meditation feels, the psychological and physiological effects of meditation, and the instructions for a number of meditations.

Listen to Relaxing Music

Listening to music that is relaxing to you, at work or at home, can help you maintain a positive, productive frame of mind. Some of my clients have put a radio in their office, tuned to their favorite station with the volume set low. They have found this keeps them relaxed, productive, and enhances enjoyment of their work.

Center Yourself on Your Guiding Values Every Morning

Centering is another way to calm, clear, and focus your mind. Centering is a form of guided meditation that allows you to let go of your everyday concerns for a few minutes in order to get back in touch with your inner self—the real you. The centering technique gives you access to the immense peace and power that resides within you.

Tom Crum, in his book *The Magic of Conflict*, says, "We have all experienced the centered state. It occurs when the mind, body, and spirit become fully integrated in dynamic balance and connectedness with the world around us. There is a heightened awareness and sensitivity, a feeling that everything is perfect the way it is. The truth of who we are as human beings is revealed."

Centering means becoming one with the universe in the present moment. You can make clear distinctions between your centered (balanced) state and your uncentered (out-of-balance) state. It is impossible to be angry, fearful, or at the mercy of any conflict when you are centered. It's hard not to smile when you're truly centered. The centered state can be described by words associated with peak experiences: wholeness, aliveness,

richness, simplicity, beauty, goodness, uniqueness, effortless-
ness, playfulness, truth. It is a joyful and liberating experience.
It allows you to be more authentic, sensitive, and open.

Being centered is a state of being (not thinking or doing).
Being centered profoundly affects your way of thinking and
doing. Being centered is empowering. And to be centered or
not is your choice, at any time.

It has a positive effect not only on you but also on your
relationship to the world around you, and consequently on
how others relate to you. The environment around you literally
feels the positive influence.

In *The Genius Within You*, Alexander Everett proclaims that
if you take just fifteen minutes each day (about 1 percent of
each day) to center yourself, you'll have a profound affect on
the other 99 percent of your day.

Choose to be centered. Choose to live your life centered
on who you really are, the stable, never-changing, inner you,
the you that's reflected in your enduring guiding values. The
trick is to still your body, mind, and emotions long enough to
get in touch with your inner self. Each morning, find a quiet
place, get relaxed, and center yourself on your primary mission
in life and your guiding values. Use your Command and
Control Center to help, since it describes the life you truly
want and the kind of person you want to be every day.
Visualize yourself living out the events of the day in harmony
with your guiding values. Use this centering technique as your
daily wake-up ritual and carry the resulting peaceful and
powerful state of mind with you all day long. Periodically
throughout the day, take a few minutes to recapture your state
of centeredness.

One thing that stress does is knock you off center and out
of focus. That leads to your being out of balance, not thinking
clearly, not feeling well, or feeling scared. One of the truest
tests of centeredness is whether you can maintain it while
relating to others in stressful situations. If people are afraid
and uncentered, they lose eye contact with others. If you can
stay centered and maintain eye contact with others while you
communicate, your relationships will have more depth and
clarity.

Center yourself every day on your primary mission and your guiding values and you will be a cool, calm, confident, positive, productive, and healthy person—for life.

And That's Okay

Calm your mind and regain control of it when you feel angry or worried by acknowledging what you feel and then saying, "And that's okay." For example, if you are worried about a big meeting that's coming up tomorrow, say to yourself, "I'm worried about tomorrow's meeting . . . and that's okay." If you are angry with someone because he or she let you down, say to yourself, "I'm feeling angry at Joe . . . and that's okay."

When you use this technique, you show that you are aware of your emotional state and acknowledge that it's okay to be experiencing what you are experiencing because you are a human being. And then something interesting happens: the emotion tends to disappear. That's because you are *expressing* your feelings and drawing that stress energy out of your system, letting it dissipate in a natural and more controlled manner.

If you don't acknowledge your emotional state, you get caught up in it. You let it eat away at you. Or you resist it with "I said I am not angry!" By resisting you make it stronger. In either case, the stress energy stays with you longer to possibly harm you. But by taking the role of a bystander for just a few seconds, and observing how you feel, acknowledging that feeling, and saying it's okay to feel that way, you are in control of yourself and the situation you are in.

Schedule Some Quiet Time to Think

How often have you said, "I don't even have time to think"? If that's a problem for you, then schedule some time to think. If you have the luxury of a private office, one way to calm your mind so that you can think clearly is to close your door, sit back in your chair, put your feet up on the desk (or pull out and use a drawer if that's more comfortable for you), and relax. Maybe clasp your hands behind your head, take a few cleansing breaths, and gaze out the window, if you have one, or focus your mind on something pleasant. This relaxes the strain on your mind, allows you to regain control of it, and really helps free up your creativity. Relax your mind so it can *work* for you.

If you don't have a private office, find someplace where you can quiet your mind and do some thinking (e.g., an empty conference room or the company library). Lacking that, schedule time for a walk and use that as your quiet thinking time.

Caution. Most corporate cultures have strong unwritten laws prohibiting this kind of behavior. Taking time to sit back, relax your mind, get your mental juices flowing, and do some *creative* problem solving can be dangerous. Some companies consider it heretical, lazy, and quite unbecoming. Many employees fear that the boss might catch them "just thinking" and not really working. If your company is like this, then you may have to hide somewhere to do this.

Do One Thing at a Time

You can avoid getting mentally overwhelmed by working only on one thing at a time with total involvement and totally positive expectations of success. Don't let your mind jump to other projects, other demands, other thoughts. Stay focused on the important project you have consciously chosen to work on. Abandon all else.

Here's a great analogy that was in the "Hope Health Letter."* Think of each of the things you have to do as a small drawer in a large chest of drawers. Your job is simply to pull out one drawer at a time, deal with what's in that drawer to your satisfaction, and then push it back in. Don't think about all the drawers all the time. Concentrate on the drawer that's open before you. Once you've pushed a drawer back in, let go of it.

Know your limits with regard to how many responsibilities

*Adapted with permission from HOPE Publications, Kalamazoo, Michigan. (616) 343-0770.

you take on at one time. If you are running yourself ragged and feeling overwhelmed and out-of-control, you are undermining your effectiveness, health, and happiness. Choose what's most important and let go of the rest. Do fewer things. Do them better and enjoy them more.

Cutting back on responsibilities and projects may require some straightforward talk and negotiating with pertinent people at work and family members at home. Have the courage to stand up for what you know will make you more effective, healthier, and happier. Talk and negotiate; the benefits for you, your organization, and your family are worth it.

Most corporations make a serious mistake in giving their hardworking executives, managers, and professionals far more work than they can do, let alone do well. They give people "impossible jobs," as Peter Drucker pointed out years ago. And then they wonder why everything doesn't get done, why everything isn't communicated, why quality and service are so poor, and why morale is low. Overwhelming employees with work is unhealthy for both the organization and the people. Unfortunately, this situation has become more prevalent with all the mergers and downsizings and calls for greater productivity.

To preserve your effectiveness and maximize your contributions, you should learn how to say no to activities and assignments that would overwhelm your productive capacity. Here's one effective way to do it:

> When I was Director of University Relations at a large university, I hired a very talented, proactive, creative writer. One day, after he had been on the job for a few months, I went into his office and asked him to work on some urgent matters that were pressing on me.
>
> He said, "Stephen, I'll do whatever you want me to do. Just let me share with you my situation."
>
> Then he took me over to his wallboard, where he had listed over two dozen projects he was working on, together with performance criteria and deadline dates that had been clearly negotiated before. He was highly disciplined, which is why I went to see him in the first place. "If you want to get something done, give it to a busy man."

Then he said, "Stephen, to do the jobs that you want done right would take several days. Which of these projects would you like to delay or cancel to satisfy your request?"

Well, I didn't want to take the responsibility for that. I didn't want to put a cog in the wheel of one of the most productive people on the staff just because I happened to be managing by crisis at the time. The jobs I wanted done were urgent, but not important. So I went and found another crisis manager and gave the job to him.*

Recommended Resources

Covey, Stephen. *The Seven Habits of Highly Effective People.* New York: Fireside, 1989.

Crum, Thomas. *The Magic of Conflict.* New York: Simon & Schuster, 1987.

Harp, David. *The New Three-Minute Meditator.* Oakland, Calif.: New Harbinger, 1990.

LeShan, Lawrence. *How to Meditate.* Boston: Little, Brown & Co., 1974.

Miller, Emmett. *Letting Go of Stress.* Audiocassette. Stanford, Calif.: Source Cassette Learning Systems, 1980.

————. *Relaxation and Inspiration: Beyond Stress to Inner Peace and Power.* Videocassette. Stanford, Calif.: Source Cassette Learning Systems, 1985.

I CALM MY MIND,
CENTER MYSELF,
AND THINK CLEARLY UNDER PRESSURE
EVERY DAY.

---

*Stephen Covey. *The Seven Habits of Highly Effective People.* New York: Fireside, 1989, page 157.

9

Choose to Be Physically Tough and Full of Energy

Unleash the power in your body.

If you want to have the energy to make significant contributions at work, at home, and in your community, if you want to *enjoy* life unhampered by chronic fatigue, illness, disease, or disability, then choose to be physically tough and full of energy. Daily Power Choice 4 keeps your body properly fueled and fine-tuned so it can help you create and enjoy the kind of life you truly want.

> *"When health is absent, wisdom cannot reveal itself, art cannot become manifest, strength cannot be exerted, wealth is useless and reason is powerless."*
>
> —Herophilies

How It Works

Your body is one of the three components—body, mind, spirit—of your personal effectiveness, or your ability to produce desired results. Did you ever notice what happens to your personal effectiveness when your body is out of shape, injured, sick, diseased, tired, or just plain not healthy? But when you are healthy and fit, you are on top of the world. You are ready for action and able to tackle anything. You take on projects that less fit people think are impossible. You eat problems for breakfast and overcome obstacles without breaking stride. You do more with less effort. You've got the energy and stamina you need to put forth the extra effort that makes all the difference between success and failure, or between satisfactory and unbelievable!

When you have that "I feel great" feeling, you feel good about yourself, your self-confidence is high, and you feel more loving toward others. And the people you come in contact with are inspired and won over by your positive energy, your vigor, your happy disposition, and your action orientation.

Physical health is a state in which all body systems (nervous, muscular, skeletal, circulatory, digestive, immune, hormonal) are working in an optimal way. *Physical fitness* is the physical ability to perform a physical task. It's possible to be healthy in general but not physically fit for a specific activity. Does it make sense to you to be "pretty healthy" but not fit enough to really enjoy activities with family and friends or a sport you like? Imagine the possibilities that open up for you if you are fit to engage in all the activities you really would like to try.

Being healthy and fit are key factors in determining the quality of your life. You want to keep your body well maintained and fueled for success, so that it will support rather than interfere with or even prevent your productive efforts and enjoyment of life. Wise physical activity and wise eating habits give you the sustained energy, mental clarity, and positive mental attitude you need to produce the results you want— and the opportunity to enjoy them.*

The easiest way to unleash the power in your body is to be physically active and eat wisely on a daily basis. Fortunately, your activity level and eating habits (and thus your fitness level and health) are two things you can control almost totally every day! It's just a matter of making choices and taking action.

It's Your Choice

Make a deep-down choice right now about what kind of physical condition you want to be in for the rest of your life.

*The information in this section is not intended as a substitute for professional health care. You should consult pertinent health professionals before making any significant changes in your health-related behavior.

☐　I choose to be physically tough, resilient to stress and strain, energetic, full of stamina, in shape, and in control of my weight.

☐　I choose to be physically weak, unable to withstand much stress and strain, always tired and low on energy, lacking in stamina, overweight and out of shape, and a good candidate for a heart attack or some other serious health problem.

Wise Supporting Actions

I hope you had the energy to choose option 1. Here are some specific actions that will make you physically tough and full of energy.

Move, Strengthen, and Stretch Your Body

"If exercise came in a pill bottle, it would be the most widely prescribed 'medicine' by far."

—unknown

Regular, moderate physical activity is essential, especially if you live a sedentary life. A sedentary life-style is a real killer. So, move it or lose it! A body in motion tends to stay in motion. A body not in motion tends to stay that way—and tends to atrophy and deteriorate. This deterioration happens quite rapidly, as anyone who has been immobilized (broken arm or leg) or bedridden can testify.

Your lifelong fitness program should focus on your heart and lung capacities, your muscular strength, your flexibility, and on your having fun. A workout (or physical fun time) that addresses all of these effectively can easily be done in forty to sixty minutes and can include:

- Warm up and mild stretching (5 minutes)
- Aerobic activity (20–30 minutes)
- Muscle-strengthening activity (5–15 minutes)
- Cool down and stretching (10 minutes)

How frequently? Every other day is fine for a physical fun time such as the one just outlined. As you get more fit, you can increase your minutes of aerobic and/or muscle-strengthening activity.

Exercising the same muscle group every day can lead to trouble, so it's important to either alternate days of exercise and rest, or alternate muscle-group workouts (e.g., jog one day, swim the next), or just do a lighter, slower workout on the in-between day.

And let's put the time involved into perspective right now. One hour out of forty-eight hours is roughly 2 percent of your time. If you engage in one hour of healthy physical activity every other day, that 2 percent of your time will have extraordinary impact on the other 98 percent of your time. Your return on investment will be absolutely incredible.

What's the best time to exercise? It's your choice. Experiment to see what works best for you. According to the Hope Heart Institute, here are some things to consider:

Before Breakfast

• Is "out of the way" and not subject to being displaced by things that "come up" during the day.
• Clears the fog so you can begin your day refreshed and alert.
• Is easily followed by a shower.
• If done outside, gives you a chance to enjoy the peace and beauty of the early morning.

Before Lunch

• Enables you to work off morning tensions.
• Can help curb your lunch appetite.
• Refreshes you to meet afternoon demands.

Before Dinner

• Clears the day's tensions.
• Helps you avoid "just home from the office" binges and snacking.

* Can help curb your dinner appetite.
* Refreshes you for evening activities.

Before Bed

* Can help you relax and clear your mind of the day's problems so you can sleep soundly.*

You should not exercise when suffering from an acute infection (a common cold is just that). Also do not exercise if you have the flu, an intestinal upset, or other virus. If you have a fever, don't exercise for twenty-four hours after your temperature returns to normal; resume at a slower pace than before your illness.

Here are some guidelines for moving, strengthening, and stretching your body effectively:

1. **Pumping air.** Aerobic exercise is the one to choose when you want the most benefit in the least time. Almost any physical activity that makes your heart and lungs work moderately hard will do the job: walking, cycling, jogging, rowing, exercycling, swimming, cross-country skiing, dancing, stair climbing, rope skipping. Other activities that can be beneficial aerobically *if* the action keeps your heart rate elevated: basketball, racquetball, singles tennis, squash, soccer.

Effective aerobic exercise must be something you *enjoy*. It must be done regularly (every other day), at a sustained level (at least 20 to 30 minutes), and moderately vigorous (to elevate your heart rate to about 65 to 90 percent of its maximum rate, according to the American College of Sports Medicine).

Enjoy a variety of aerobic activities so that you can switch from one to another whenever boredom threatens. This switching also helps prevent overuse of a particular muscle group.

One way to see if your aerobic activity is vigorous enough but not too vigorous is the "talk test." You should be able to carry on a conversation without huffing and puffing. If you are breathless, slow down. Another way is to monitor your heart

*Adapted with permission from HOPE Publications, Kalamazoo, Michigan. (616) 343-0700.

rate. Calculate your target heart-rate zone (in heart beats per minute) by subtracting your age from 220 and taking 65 and 90 percent of that figure. Your heart rate (pulse) should be within this zone throughout your workout.

Use the first five minutes or so to stretch and warm up before your workout. This helps minimize injury and it feels great. And take ten minutes afterward to stretch and cool down.

What about jogging? According to Dr. Ken Cooper, the author and expert on jogging and aerobic exercise, people who jog for overall fitness should not do more than a ten-minute mile. A faster pace won't contribute much to fitness and will increase the risk of injury. Dr. Cooper recommends a minimum of two miles a day at this pace, four days a week, or a maximum of three miles a day, five days a week. As a general rule, when you feel you can do more exercise, extend your time rather than increase your pace. You'll get more benefit from running slowly for a longer time than you will from running faster and quitting sooner.

Many fitness professionals believe walking at a brisk pace is the ideal aerobic exercise because it provides great fitness benefits with low risk of injury. No special equipment is needed other than a pair of well-cushioned, comfortable shoes. By just walking one hour a day at 4 m.p.h. you can lose up to thirty-six pounds in one year (without making *any* changes in your diet)! So get out there and walk your buns off. Not only will you reduce your bun size, you will reduce your waist size and feel terrific. And you can chat with a friend while you walk or listen to your Walkman.

The idea is to enjoy a moderate level of physical activity on a regular basis. It need not be a formal exercise program. Mowing the lawn, working in the yard or garden, and other activities are fine as long as they provide sustained, moderate effort on a regular basis. Beware of easy chairs, couches, TVs, and other objects that encourage an excessively sedentary, self-destructive life-style. Whenever you are faced with the take charge point of being physically inactive or physically active, take charge of your life and choose to be active. Also look for opportunities throughout the day to move your body—opportunities to sneak in some exercise. Use the stairway instead of the elevator. Park at the far end of the lot and enjoy the longer walk.

2. **Muscle-strengthening exercises and activities.** In your physical fun time, include activities that tone your muscles, increase their strength and endurance, improve your posture, and increase lean body mass. Each major muscle group (legs, arms, abdomen, back, chest) should be tuned up regularly. You can use special equipment at fitness centers, inexpensive weights at home, or just the resistance of your own muscles or body weight.

Two good strengthening exercises are the half situp and the knee pushup. The *half situp* (or crunch) is good for your stomach and back muscles (only three minutes of crunches a day will contribute significantly to a flat and firm stomach). Lie on your back with legs together, knees bent, feet flat on floor, hands across your chest, and chin close to chest. *Slowly* curl just your head and shoulders off the floor. Then slowly roll back to the floor. To reduce the risk of back injury, keep your lower back *flat* on the floor. Do not do situps with legs straight.

Knee pushups are great for your shoulders, arms, and chest (especially your pecs). Lie facedown with legs together and knees on the floor. Keeping your knees on the floor to reduce the risk of low back injury, push your upper body off the floor until arms are fully extended. Do not hold your breath during this or any exercise. Add variety by varying how far apart you spread your arms. Also try this with your elbows right next to your body.

These exercises do not require a lot of time—maybe a few minutes. The benefits of having a stronger body (and flatter stomach) are well worth the effort.

An excellent reference for strengthening exercises is *Getting Stronger* by Bill Pearl (see Recommended Resources at the end of this chapter). It is fully illustrated, with general conditioning exercises for people of all ages and for twenty-one sports, with cross-references to free weights, Nautilus, and Universal machines. It also includes a specific routine for deskbound, white-collar workers.

3. **Stretching.** Stretching is simply movement that extends or expands your muscles—muscles that may have cramped or tightened from stress or prolonged inactivity. Regular stretching makes your muscles more elastic and less susceptible to cramping and spasm. It increases your range of motion, prevents injuries, increases coordination, and energizes you. You will also be more flexible, able to engage in more vigorous physical activity easily and with less danger of injury.

Stretching is easy and feels really good when done correctly. It is peaceful, relaxing, and noncompetitive. Unfortunately, few people know how to stretch properly. The idea is not to see how far you can stretch (which often leads to injury), but to stay within your comfort zone and away from the idea that the more it hurts, the more you get out of it.

Here are some guidelines for stretching properly and safely:

- Stretch with slow and gentle movements; *never* bounce.
- Listen to your body and stay within your safe stretch zone; do not cause pain. Do not exceed about 70 percent of your maximum possible stretch; if you stretch too far, your muscle will try to save itself and contract—the opposite of what you want.
- Exhale slowly as you stretch.
- Stretch according to how it feels. If it feels good, you are doing it right.

When should you stretch? Stretching is a great way to make the transition from the sedentary parts of your day to the physically active parts. (Just ask your cat or dog.) Stretch after rising in morning (do some knee pushups and half situps while you're at it). Stretch anytime during the day to relieve built up muscular tension and the aches and pains of inactivity. And, of course, stretch before and after strenuous activity. And you can stretch anywhere, including in your office.

Obtain a copy of *Stretching* by Bob Anderson (see Recommended Resources at end of chapter). It's an excellent, illustrated guide on how to stretch properly. It contains stretches for everyday fitness, for relaxation, and for walking, running, golf, tennis, racquetball, skiing, cycling, soccer, basketball, and other sports.

Why should regular physical activity be part of your life-long strategy for personal effectiveness—and a daily priority? Your health is one of your most important assets. Most of us don't realize this *until* we have a health problem, then the extraordinary value of good health becomes quite clear. It's easy to get so caught up in the demands of your job and family that you feel you just don't have time for physical activity. Your lifelong desire to be vibrant and healthy gets neglected as you scramble to meet the short-term demands of your everyday life.

Beware. Neglecting to take care of yourself *daily* is dangerous. What good is it to get everything done on today's To Do list if you sacrifice your health in the process or even die of a heart attack? Ask yourself: Is there anything I'm doing at work that is worth losing my health for or worth dying for? Not likely. But many executives, managers, and professionals lead their everyday life as if that were the case. They undermine their health, their happiness, and their effectiveness in the process. They are killing themselves as well as the quality of their lives.

So on those busy days when you are tempted to put off your revitalization through physical activity, remind yourself of the crucial role it plays in your commitment to lead and enjoy a healthy and productive life. Treat yourself right. Make regular, moderate physical activity one of the nice things you do for yourself. Something as simple as a twenty-minute walk every other day can yield a tremendous return on a minimal investment of your time and effort.

Say what? You can't find twenty minutes out of forty-eight hours to take a walk? All right. Let's hear your excuses.*

Excuse 1. I don't have time. I don't suspect you have time for a heart attack, either. Or time to be sick, to drag yourself

*Adapted with permission from HOPE Publications, Kalamazoo, Michigan. (616) 343-0700.

through the day with no energy, to be depressed, or to feel bloated, fat, and awkward in your movement.

I have found that executives, managers, and professionals who say they don't have time for regular, moderate physical activity are the ones who need it most. One reason they don't have time is because they are out of control. They are not making wise choices or taking wise actions when it comes to taking good care of themselves so they can maintain their ability to be effective and productive.

Not being able to find twenty minutes for some moderately vigorous physical activity every other day is a copout. It's denying your body what it needs to operate effectively. Your body needs food and water, and your body *needs* exercise.

Here's how to find the time. *Choose* to have the time. It's as simple as that. At the beginning of each week, schedule your physical fun time for the week as a high-priority item. Then fit the rest of your work and family activities around those tune-up times. Take pride in working through difficult situations at work (e.g., mergers, downsizings, reorganizations, important projects) without ever missing your physical fun time and without ever sacrificing your health for the crisis of the moment. Treat yourself right. Exercise faithfully!

Don't have time? Eliminate one or two TV programs and you've got an hour. Use your exercycle before dinner as you watch the evening news. You can get in your day's exercise, eliminate built-up stress, curb your appetite, and catch up on world affairs all at the same time! Or, instead of taking twenty minutes to read the same old items in the newspaper every day, take a brisk walk. Or read the paper or a good book when you use the exercycle.

Make time to exercise. Put it on your daily calendar and give it top priority. (Do you get the feeling I think this is really important? Good, because it is. It can make a *huge* difference in your life!)

Excuse 2. It's not convenient. You can make it very convenient. Enjoy your physical fun time at work if your company has a place to walk or a fitness center. Exercise at home (equipment is not necessary but is available). Exercise on trips—most hotels have exercise rooms and equipment. You can always exercise in your hotel room or run up and down the emergency stairway. You can always go for a walk.

Excuse 3. It's too expensive. It does not have to be expensive at all. You can do everything you need to do right at home. The only equipment you may need is a good pair of comfortable shoes to walk in.

Excuse 4. I'm not athletic. You don't have to be athletic. You only have to be able to move your body and give your heart and lungs a good workout.

Excuse 5. I don't have the energy. Exercise *creates* energy. People who exercise regularly do so because it makes them feel good afterward. Many times I've dragged myself to the fitness center, tired out and just wanting to go home and collapse. But after my workout I'm refreshed, revitalized, and always feel much better.

Excuse 6. I always get sore. Forget "no pain, no gain." Avoid discomfort and take it easy. Don't do too much, too soon. Start a routine of exercising every other day and gradually increase the length of your workout rather than the intensity.

Excuse 7. It's too much work to get in shape. Simply adjust the pace or intensity of your exercise so that it suits you. Find a steady pace that will allow you to exercise for twenty continuous minutes with *pleasure.*

Excuse 8. I'm not interested in fitness. I've got other things to worry about. Regular exercise reduces frustration, aggression, and depression. It gives you a sense of well-being that has a positive impact on all areas of your life. It's not unusual for difficult problems to solve themselves during an exercise session—the result of clearer thinking and unleashed creativity, typical byproducts of exercise.

Excuse 9. I've tried getting more exercise before, but I never stick with it. Well, you can this time. Twenty minutes, every other day. No big deal. If necessary, commit to exercising with a buddy or put gold stars on a calendar every day you exercise. Or schedule it on your daily planner at the beginning of each week, make it a top priority, and put a big check mark by it after each exercise session.

Make it an essential habit, like eating and sleeping (because it *is* essential). Go back to the beginning of this chapter and look at the deep-down choice you made. Do you really want to choose option 2? The key to sticking with option 1 is making a *deep-down* personal commitment because that is what you truly want. Keep that promise to yourself in front of you *daily*. (It'll be in your Personal Effectiveness Plan.)

Excuse 10. I feel guilty about taking the time to exercise. Regular exercise is necessary for good health. Your body needs it. Exercise provides you with the energy and positive disposition you need to enjoy life and to contribute effectively to the other important people in your life. Do yourself a favor and do the other people in your life a favor: exercise regularly.

Excuse 11. I hate exercise. It's boring. Make it interesting and exciting. Choose an exercise that's fun for you. If you hate aerobic dancing, don't do it. Find alternatives that you do enjoy. It doesn't have to be "exercise." Any moderately intense physical activity sustained for twenty minutes will do. Sing and dance as you clean the house for twenty minutes. Be creative.

If you hate exercising alone, do it with a friend or join a health club where you can exercise and socialize. If you hate exercising with other people, do it in the privacy of your own home with your favorite music blasting. If you like being outside, do it outside. Add variety. Then go for a brisk walk on Monday, jump on your exercycle in front of the TV on Wednesday, and go for a swim with a friend on Friday.

Enjoy the moment and the movement! Experience your exercising with all your senses. Focus on feeling the movement throughout your body. Feel the temperature, the breeze, the smell of the outdoors; observe the wide variety of colors and textures in your environment; listen to all the sounds; enjoy moving through the air, through the water.

If it makes you feel special, buy attractive sportswear or a nice piece of exercise equipment, or special music and headphones. If such things will make exercising more enjoyable and fun for you, and facilitate your exercising regularly, get them.

Many of you will want to start an exercise program after reading this section on the benefits of physical activity. You will go out and start exercising. That's wonderful. Do it. Just don't overdo it. Be patient and take it easy. You can't go from out of shape to in shape in three days.

Make being healthy and fit *a way of life!* The rewards you will enjoy and the pain and illness you will avoid make it well worth your investment in a little physical activity each day. You may want to consider making "physical fun time" one of your hobbies!

Make Wise Choices Regarding What You Put in Your Body

Here's a gold mine of opportunities to make wise choices and take wise actions. A plethora of take charge points where you can make choices and take actions that keep your body lean, energetic, and resilient to stress and health problems. As a bonus, you can end up eating 25 percent *less* food, and saving at least that much on your food budget. Once you know what constitutes a healthy, low-fat diet, you can consciously choose foods that sustain your energy level and promote a calm mental clarity. You'll avoid foods that either give you nervous jitters or a depressing sluggishness, and that make your energy level go up and down like a roller coaster.

Here are some *unwise food choices*—bad fuel for your body.

• *Fat.* Fat in food causes fat in you, so limit your eating of foods high in fat. A food is considered high in fat if more than 25 percent of its calories are derived from fat. Packaged foods high in fat can be identified easily and, therefore, avoided. Just read the label and:

1. Multiply the grams of fat per serving by 9 (there are 9 calories in each gram of fat).
2. Divide the result by the number of calories per serving.
3. Multiply by 100 to get the percentage of calories from fat.

Whenever you find a high-fat food in your hand, you have a clear take charge point. Do you choose to be fit or to be fat?

It's your choice. When it comes to adding weight to your body, fat is fat, whether it's saturated or unsaturated, animal or vegetable. According to the Hope Heart Institute, the most common high-fat foods are cream and things made with cream, cheese, butter or margarine (both are almost pure fat) and things made with them, whole milk and things made with whole milk, fatty meats, canned meats, lunch meats, sausage, vegetable oils and animal shortening and things made with them, nuts, avocados, mayonnaise. High-fat foods can make you drowsy, and when consumed in large portions can put you to sleep.

• *Refined sugar.* A sweet treat may pick you up, but soon thereafter it may also make your blood-sugar level plunge, leaving you worse off in terms of energy, mood, and hunger. Dr. John Yacenda, writing in *Fitness Management,* says that if you use sugar to raise your energy level, you are "pumping air into a tire with a hole in it—just as sure as you pump it up, it will go back down." Continually eating sweets stimulates hunger and reduces your activity level.

• *Caffeine.* Minimize your caffeine consumption. It can cause "the jitters," insomnia, irritability, and anxiety. It can also affect blood sugar and secretion of stomach acids. Drinks high in caffeine turn sugars into body fat. Caffeine can be addictive. You may experience withdrawal symptoms if you stop cold turkey, and you may have headaches for one to three days. Cut back gradually.

Note that it is not necessarily a matter of eliminating all the unwise foods from your life. It's more a matter of consciously choosing to eat *more* of the foods that will do a whole lot more for you. The problem is that under stress, we make poor choices regarding what and how much we eat. And the stomach does not digest well when we are stressed.

Here are some *wise food choices*—good fuel for your body. These foods give you sustained energy, promote a calm alertness, and make you feel great physically and mentally. They enhance your personal effectiveness and your enjoyment of life. It just feels good to eat right.

1. The current guidelines for wise nutrition are to limit fat to no more than 25 percent of total calories consumed each day (every low-fat meal is a victory for you). Limit protein to 15 percent of total calories. Increase complex carbohydrates to 60 percent of total calories. Limit total calories per day to the amount required to maintain your ideal weight—about 10 to 25 calories per pound depending on your activity level and metabolism rate (e.g., if you are inactive, multiply your *desired*—not actual—weight by 10 to determine how many calories you need each day). Limit cholesterol to 300 mg per day and sodium to not more than 3,000 mg per day. Increase fiber to 25 to 35 grams per day.

2. Drink water. About 60 percent of the body's weight is water. Water is essential for proper functioning of every cell in your body, helps cleanse your body of impurities, and contributes to mental sharpness. You can survive for weeks without food; you can survive only a few days without water.

Most people need 6 to 8 cups (64 ounces) of water (water, juices, milk) daily, spaced throughout the day. Caffeinated drinks don't count because they increase your thirst. Hot weather and physical activity also increase your need for water.

3. Eat complex carbohydrates for sustained energy. Increase your consumption of foods like potatoes, whole-grain breads and cereals, pasta, rice (rice is about 87 percent complex carbohydrate, an excellent choice), legumes (dried beans and peas), and fresh vegetables and fruits.

4. Eat small portions (2 to 4 ounces) of low-fat protein for growth, repair of your body, and mental alertness. Foods like lean meat, fish, poultry without the skin, and nonfat dairy products are high in protein and low in fat. Watch your portions. Excess protein is converted to body fat.

It is not necessary to count calories, grams of fat, carbohydrates, or protein. By eating reasonable portions of vegetables, whole-grains, fruits, legumes, pasta, and small portions of low-fat protein, you will automatically follow the basic guidelines for wise nutrition. Fresh fruits and vegetables are also good sources of vitamins, minerals, and fiber.

Wise Eating Habits

1. **Eat with a positive purpose.** To be healthy, to have an alert but calm mind, to have sustained energy for high performance, to maximize your good moods and minimize your irritable, depressed, sluggish moods, to enjoy permanent weight control—whatever your particular purpose may be, keep it in mind as you plan your meals every day. Lock in at least two low-fat meals each day by having a set menu and/or knowing exactly what you are going to eat.

2. **Only eat when hungry.** Only eat when your body is calling for food. Don't eat when you are not hungry. Don't eat just for something to do, out of habit, or because the clock says it's time to eat.

3. **Watch those portions.** Slow down, relax, and savor each bite. Learn to sense when you feel about 70 percent full and stop eating at that point *before* you feel stuffed. Give your body a chance to respond to the food, to "catch up" and give you accurate feedback on how full you are. Then wait five minutes after you finish your meal before you start looking for that final sweet treat to fill you up. Better yet, get up immediately and go for a walk or get involved in something so you will forget all about your "sweet tooth."

4. **Control your environment.** This really makes wise eating easy! Do not bring unhealthy food (bad fuel) into your house. Eliminate the temptations. Kill the possibility of an accidental confrontation with an unwise food. Have lots of low-fat or no-fat foods readily available (e.g., fruits and vegetables).

5. **Experiment with food.** Find out what kind and what amount of food agrees with you and how frequently during the day you need to eat so you can stay trim and feel light, yet have plenty of energy.

6. **Minimize eating as a reward or for stress relief.** (A moment on the lips, forever on the hips!) Reward yourself with nonfood pleasures. Relieve your stress with one of the effective techniques in this book.

7. **Choose the consequences of the food as well as the food.** (You pick up both ends of the stick!) If you eat *X* food

item, you *know* it will do Y to your body or mind. Don't kid yourself. Don't mess with cause-and-effect.

8. **Don't diet.** Don't abstain from food when you are truly hungry. If you do, your body will think you are trying to starve it and, in self-defense, will decrease its metabolism rate and increase the storage of fat. Instead, to lose weight, make wise food choices and use wise eating habits, and graduallly exercise more each day. Burn more calories than you consume or consume fewer calories than you burn, or both.

9. **Eat powerfully.** To stay mentally sharp throughout your afternoon, eat a low-fat, high-protein "power lunch" of fish, lean meat, or skinless poultry, whole-grain bread or roll, and fresh fruit or vegetable. Avoid butter, rich sauces, creamy salad dressings, mayonnaise, and anything breaded or fried. Remember portion control!

10. **Rid yourself of unwise eating habits.** Associate your consumption of foods that make you fat, irritable, and sluggish with painful, ugly, smelling, gagging images of rotting food so that whenever you see or even think about these unhealthy foods you will trigger these images and thus want to maintain a healthy distance. (My thanks to Anthony Robbins for this unappealing but extremely effective technique. See *Personal Power* in Recommended Resources at end of chapter.)

Associate your consumption of foods that keep you lean and supply you with sustained energy and positive moods with images that give you wonderful feelings of pleasure, warmth, love, high self-esteem, good looks, self-confidence, delicious taste, and personal power so that these foods will be the only ones you will want to put in your body.

Let go of your excuses for not fueling up wisely. I know. You have excuses for not eating wisely. Let's get rid of them for good.

Excuse 1. I don't have time to eat healthy foods. Many healthy foods require zero preparation (fresh fruits and vegetables). They are ready for instant consumption. Other healthy foods require no more preparation than other foods and probably less preparation since you don't have to prepare fattening sauces or other accompaniments.

There are a number of ways you can speed up meal preparation. Crockpots give you a nutritious meal that's ready when you get home. Modern ovens have timing features so that your meal is cooked just as you arrive home. Complete dinners can be prepared on the weekend, put on plates, and frozen so that during the week you can pop them in a microwave and be eating within minutes. Some meals can be prepared in bulk (soups, salads), refrigerated, and be readily available for healthy meals during the week.

You can also find commercially prepared convenience foods at your grocery store that meet the nutritional guidelines and aren't high in salt, sugar, or fat (read the labels closely). And the next time you consider grabbing a quick bite at a fast-food restaurant, go to the fresh produce section of a grocery store instead for something that's ready to eat, good for you, cheap, and convenient.

Excuse 2. Healthy food is not tasty. Since you have probably been eating a lot of unwise foods for a long time, your taste buds have adapted to the sweet or fatty taste of those foods. Wise foods may taste funny or different for a short while. But if you gradually increase your consumption of wise foods and decrease your consumption of unwise foods, your taste buds will adjust to the healthier foods. You will find that your new, healthier foods are now very tasty. Your former junk foods will now taste weird—far too sweet, far too rich.

Excuse 3. I'm overweight and I can't control my eating habits. You *can* be lean and you *can* control your eating habits. It's a matter of making choices and taking action that supports those choices. The following section describes the keys to lifelong weight control.

Effective, Lifelong Weight Control

For most of us, being overfat is primarily a result of our sedentary life-style and an overconsumption of high-fat foods, and just plain eating too much food. To lose fat, you need to be more active and eat less fatty food. A realistic and safe rate of weight loss is about one to two pounds per week. (By the way, body fat is a better indicator to monitor than weight. You may want to measure your progress via inches rather than pounds.) Think *gradual* fat loss, not quick fat loss! Gradual fat loss is based on wise choices regarding what you eat and increased physical activity, not on starving your body.

Here are the five keys to effective, permanent fat control.

Key 1. A deep-down, personal choice. The only way for you to be lean, energetic, and healthy for the rest of your life is for you to make that choice of your own free will without pressure. If you truly desire to have your fat under control for the rest of your life, then you will be willing to do what needs to be done to make it happen. If you truly do *not* want all the social, physical, emotional, and health problems associated with being overfat, the supporting actions are much, much easier to take. Once you recognize that what you need is a lifelong commitment, not a quick fix, you will start making wise eating choices consistently. And in this case, slow and steady wins the race.

Key 2. Motivational imagery. It is important that you have two very clear, sensory-rich images of yourself: one that shows your current reality as overfat, sluggish, out of breath, tired, visually unappealing (an actual photograph of you—all of you—can be quite effective), and one in which you can see yourself the way you want to be—lean, firm, active, attractive, energetic, strong. Find an actual photograph of the slim, trim you of yesteryear, or use a picture of someone from a magazine who has the kind of body you choose to have. If you don't have actual pictures, just use mental images. Take a good look at both images daily and choose the one you truly desire, then take actions that support that choice. (See *The New Neuropsychology of Weight Control* by Steven DeVore in Recommended Resources at the end of this chapter. This is a well-researched, well-presented weight control program on eight audiocassettes plus workbook. It has an excellent record of success and will help you apply what you learn here.)

Key 3. Exercise. Regular exercise is an essential factor in achieving permanent fat control. The most beneficial exercise for fat loss and fat control is done regularly (preferably daily), works the large leg muscles, is of moderate intensity, and is of thirty to sixty minutes in duration.

Walking with moderate intensity will work just fine, as will jogging, cycling, swimming, aerobic dancing, and the use of some exercise equipment such as an exercycle, treadmill, rowing machine, or stairclimber.

Key 4. Relaxation and behavior modification. If most of your overeating is stress-related behavior, use some of the relaxation techniques in Chapters 6 and 8 to regain control of yourself when you have the emotional urge (but not the physiological need) to eat (definitely a take charge point).

It's also very helpful to have a plan prepared ahead of time to deal with tempting situations. These situations might be special celebrations, visitors from out of town, holiday feasts, or the aroma wafting from your favorite bakery.

Once you identify these situations, you can mentally rehearse how you'll handle them when they arise. For example, if your favorite (and fattening) dessert is at the party, use your instant Relaxation Response: take a deep breath and say, "Relax. I don't want this. I choose to be lean and energetic." Or fill up on fresh vegetables before you go to the party so you won't be tempted to eat when you get there. Or be prepared with a compliment for the hostess: "Betty, the black forest cake looks wonderful as usual, but I'll have to take a raincheck this time."

If you know the "hungries" always attack you midmorning or midafternoon, then plan to eat some fruit you really enjoy at that take charge point. Thus, you'll prevent panic gorging of fatty foods.

When you do give in to a momentary temptation, consciously choose to do so—don't berate yourself—and then resume your wiser eating habits.

Key 5. Eat wisely. The evidence is strong that traditional dieting does not work. People lose weight and then gain it back, diet, and regain. And they are pretty miserable the whole time, feeling deprived at one moment and guilty the next.

Refer to the section on wise eating habits and wise food choices to see how you can eat wisely to lose fat and keep it off permanently. And keeping a food diary—a record of everything you put in your mouth and how much—keeps you honest and helps you eat consciously and with portion control in mind.

Choose Not to Smoke

You *know* damn well that smoking is a *major* risk to your health. If you are currently smoking, you are choosing to destroy your health. You are choosing to put oxygen-robbing carbon monoxide into your body. Another lethal source of carbon monoxide is the end of your tailpipe.

You are also choosing to put nicotine into your body, which is an addictive substance and a major contributor to cardiovascular disease, and cigarette tars, which form an ugly, brown, sticky mass in your lungs. And you are putting numerous other toxic and cancer-causing substances into your body.

If you haven't been living consciously and haven't read the Surgeon General's health warnings on cigarette packages, here's what they say:

- Smoking causes lung cancer, heart disease, and emphysema, and may complicate pregnancy.
- Smoking by pregnant women may result in fetal injury, premature birth, and low birth weight.
- Cigarette smoke contains carbon monoxide.
- Quitting smoking now greatly reduces serious risks to your health.

And the leaflet in packages of oral contraceptives says: "Cigarette smoking increases the risk of *serious* adverse effects on the heart and blood vessels from oral contraceptive use. This risk increases with age and with heavy smoking and is quite marked in women over 35 years of age. Women who use oral contraceptives should not smoke."

Cigarette smoking causes 30 percent of all cancer deaths. About 90 percent of lung cancer patients are smokers. Smoking also causes cancers of the larynx, esophagus, pancreas, bladder, kidney, and mouth. People who smoke stink. And so does *everything* exposed to their smoke (clothes, home, car, children, office).

By choosing not to smoke, you greatly reduce your chance of serious, if not deadly, health problems. You also reduce the air pollution wherever you happen to be, thus contributing to the health of others (including your family) instead of causing health problems for them. And you don't stink anymore.

About 40 million ex-smokers can tell you that choosing to quit was one of the wisest choices they ever made, and you will say the same thing.

There's no one best way to stop smoking. Some people just stop cold turkey; others taper off slowly. Some find quit-smoking groups helpful, while others find stop-smoking audiocassette programs effective. To explore your options, contact your local chapter of the American Lung Association or the American Cancer Society, your doctor, your company's medical department or wellness program, or a local hospital's wellness program.

Regardless of what way you choose to quit, the key is making a deep-down personal commitment to be a healthy person. Once you do that, you'll find a way (commitment = action). Cigarette companies have spent billions of dollars to link smoking to glamorous things in life. Wake up. Live consciously. What smoking is really linked to is severe disability and torturous death, and that's not very glamorous. For a candid story of what heavy smoking (and no exercise and bad eating habits) can do to you, read *Mr. King, You're Having A Heart Attack* (see Recommended Resources at end of chapter).

Choose to Put Minimal, If Any, Alcohol in Your Body

Alcohol is the drug most abused in the business world. *Business Week* (March 25, 1991) reported that at least 10 percent of senior executives have an alcohol problem. The immediate negative consequences of putting excessive amounts of alcohol into your body (and brain) include:

• Loss of your ability to make wise choices and take wise actions
• Loss of control of your mental, emotional, and physical capacities and all that this can lead to (raging attacks on family members, horrifying physical and emotional abuse, and the serious lifelong impact such abuse has on the victim)
• Greatly increased chance of being involved in an accident and killing someone else
• Nearly impossible to get a *healthy* sleep at night
• If a large quantity is consumed rapidly, sudden death

The long-term negative consequences of alcohol abuse include cirrhosis of the liver; cancer of the mouth, throat, esophagus, and liver, and possibly breast cancer; obesity, gastritis, and acute pancreatis; and depression. About 25 percent of all hospitalized patients are there for an alcohol-related health problem. And, of course, booze can ruin your life in many other ways. You can lose your job, your family, your friends, and your self-respect.

If you feel you *need* to have alcohol in your life, ask yourself why. Is it to relax? The relaxation techniques in this book are far more effective and a lot healthier. Is it to have fun and be sociable? Do you mean you can't have fun and enjoy people and life without alcohol? Try it. You can! Is it because "everyone else does"? Is "everyone else" running your life (read Chapter 4 again)? Is it to drown your sorrows or to avoid dealing with a problem? Or is it just a habit that you've gotten into without understanding the potentially serious negative consequences for your success, health, and happiness?

Remember, whatever you put at the center of your life is what has power over you. If you *need* to have several drinks every day, you have put alcohol in charge of your life. Does alcohol have control over you? Are you addicted to alcohol? Can you go one month, one week, or one day without a drink? Try it and find out.

It is your choice to drink or not to drink. Don't just do it out of habit or because everyone else is doing it. Make it a conscious choice on your part. If you choose to put alcohol into your body, limit your consumption to no more than two drinks a day. And if you choose not to put alcohol into your body, with the increased health consciousness, a pleasant "no thank you" or "plain soda, please" will gain you admiration and respect.

Talk about a magnificent opportunity to make a wise choice and take a wise action! Here's an incredible chance to have a profound positive impact on your life. If you need help with your drinking problem, ask for help. Make the wise choice and take action *right now*. You can overcome this problem. Current treatment programs are very effective. Contact your medical department or employee assistance program at work, or the Alcoholics Anonymous group in your area. By seeking help, you are making a wise choice to treat yourself with respect and to take good care of yourself. Your life will be a whole lot easier and happier without alcohol.

And please never drive when you are drunk. Thousands of people are killed needlessly every year by drunk drivers; half of all auto fatalities are caused by drunk drivers. Imagine, for a moment, what it must feel like to know you killed someone *very special*—someone's father, mother, son, or daughter. Have a sober designated driver, get a ride with someone, or take a taxi.

If you are the manager of a person with an alcohol problem, contact your employee assistance people about the correct way to confront and get help for the employee. This is the only kind and responsible thing to do. You can save that person's life (as many happy, healthy, and productive recovered alcoholics will confirm). Avoiding the confrontation does not help anyone.

Heed the Warning Signs of a Heart Attack

Heart disease and stroke are the number-one causes of death in America today. If you are overweight, out of shape, stressed, and abusing your body with alcohol and cigarettes, pay close attention. You are a good candidate for a heart attack.

Here are the risk factors: stress, overweight, smoking, cholesterol level over 200, family history of heart disease, and denial or failure to recognize the symptoms of a heart attack (most people wait three hours before going to a hospital, then die). You do not have to have all the risk factors to have a heart attack.

The *classic symptoms* of a heart attack are:*

1. Uncomfortable pressure, squeezing, fullness, tightness, burning, or aching under the breastbone that lasts two minutes or more.
2. Other common places for pain to be felt, besides the chest, include neck and jaw, inside arm and shoulder (left side more frequently than right), upper abdomen (often mistaken for indigestion pain), and between the shoulder blades.
3. The pain may be continuous or may come and go.
4. Often there is shortness of breath, dizziness, weakness, clamminess, sweating, nausea, vomiting, and/or anxiety.
5. Although pain in one form or another almost always accompanies a heart attack, rather than pain, some people just have a feeling that "something is wrong." A feeling of apprehension, restlessness, or "sense of foreboding" may be recognized.

All these symptoms need not be present at the onset of a heart attack. For example, you might just have a crushing chest pain the likes of which you have never experienced before. Or you might just have a little nausea and a weird feeling.

If you are at risk, commit the classic symptoms of a heart attack to memory. And if ever you feel you might be having a heart attack, don't wait "to be sure"; get to the hospital fast. Better to have a false alarm than to be dead. (Don't you drive. Have someone take you or call an emergency squad.)

There is also a silent heart attack (silent aschemia). It's usually symptomless and painless, but it is a massive heart attack. It's antecedents—a lack of oxygen and blood flow to the

*According to the Hope Heart Institute in Seattle, Wash.

heart—can often be detected by a stress test. Ask your physician if a stress test might be appropriate for you.

Be wise. Take care of your heart. Know the risk factors and take control over the ones you *can*. For example, exercise regularly and eat wisely to keep your weight and your cholesterol and blood pressure under control, don't smoke, learn how to deal effectively with stress, pressure, and frustrations.

Have a Thorough Annual Physical Checkup

Treat yourself right. Your car probably gets an annual inspection; so should you, especially if your life subjects you to a lot of wear and tear.

And if you truly want to enjoy being as effective, healthy, and happy as you can be, don't hesitate to have a doctor check out your "I wonder if I should have a doctor look at this?" concerns. Don't procrastinate. Don't put off feeling great. Make an appointment today—right now—to get it checked out. Be in charge of your life. Be proactive. Don't wait until you are a victim.

Women, get a mammogram on a regular basis (seven out of ten women get breast cancer).

Recommended Resources

Anderson, Bob. *Stretching*. Bolinas, Calif.: Shelter Publications, 1980.

———. *Stretching—the Video*. Also a booklet, "Deskercise," for stretches you can do at your desk, and Computer Stretches software. Palmer Lake, Co.: Stretching Inc., 1987.

DeVore, Steven, Dennis Remington, Garth Fisher, Edward Parent, and Barbara Higa. *The New Neuropsychology of Weight Control*. Pleasanton, Calif.: Sybervision, 1990.

King, Larry, with B. D. Colen. *Mr. King, You're Having a Heart Attack*. New York: Delacorte Press, 1989.

Pearl, Bill. *Getting Stronger*. Bolinas, Calif.: Shelter Publications, 1986.

Robbins, Anthony. *Personal Power*. Twenty-four audiocassettes

in twelve packs of two each. Irwindale, Calif.: Guthy-
Renker Corp., 1989.

```
I CHOOSE TO BE
PHYSICALLY TOUGH
AND FULL OF ENERGY EVERY DAY.
```

10

Choose to Be Mentally Tough, Emotionally in Control, and Action Oriented

"I can do just about anything if I really put my mind to it."

If you want to use the awesome powers of your mind to *help* you make your dreams come true with maximum velocity and with minimal wasted energy and stress, then choose to be mentally focused, emotionally in control, and action oriented *every day.* This is Daily Power Choice 5—using powerful, productive mindsets.

How It Works

Your mind is one of the three components (body, mind, spirit) of your personal effectiveness. It is that part of you that looks at the world, perceives, thinks, feels, desires, believes, imagines, *creates*, makes choices, and decides to take action. Your mind is so powerful words just can't describe it.

At any given moment your mind is looking at events in a certain way, is focused on certain thoughts, is in a certain emotional state, and is inclined to make you act in a certain way. This mental and emotional state produces a certain overall *mindset* that either helps or hinders your performance. For instance, ever notice what happens when your mindset is not appropriate for the task at hand? Not very productive, are you? Maybe even counterproductive.

Daily Power Choice 5 is *consciously choosing the mindsets and the actions* that will help you produce the results you want most in your job, family, and personal life. You *can* do just about anything, if you really put your mind to it. This Daily Power Choice shows you how to "really put your mind to it." It shows you how to "program" your mind to create what you want most in your life.

You've got to have *more* than a dream to make a dream come true. You've got to have a crystal-clear picture of that dream. You've got to lock onto that desired result and take action to produce it. And you've got to have the mental toughness and emotional resilience to stay the course regardless of obstacles, opposition, or circumstances that arise. In other words, you've got to have the appropriate mindset and take the appropriate actions that will produce the result you have in mind.

What's important to know about mindsets is that you can *consciously create* them and use them as *extraordinarily powerful tools* for producing the results you want. *You can have lots of useful mindsets*—a special collection of empowering mindsets. For example:

- Your cool, calm, collected, mindset: I'm Joe Montana. It's the Superbowl. There are two minutes to go and we're down by four points. Eighty yards to go for a touchdown. No problem!
- Your holiday mindset: I am going to approach this holiday season in a calm and positive manner, and not let myself get sucked into a panicky shopping frenzy and a weight-gaining disaster. I'm going to truly enjoy the season.
- Your flexible and receptive merger mindset: I keep myself cool, calm, collected, positive, productive, and healthy as I journey through this major merger.
- Your low-stress communication mindset: I can communicate in a positive, productive, low-stress manner, even with highly emotional, out-of-control people.

You can aquire and "get into" useful mindsets in different ways. You may recall effective mindsets from your past experiences. Or you can learn powerful, productive mindsets by observing, talking to, and listening to people who have successfully produced the result you want to produce (e.g., how to run a profitable business, how to be a gold medal Olympic champion, how to be an effective parent, how to play tennis or golf well). These people can tell you what mindset is necessary to achieve results and what specific actions to take. Use them as models for effective performance.

Or you can invent your mindsets. Create a mindset and experiment with it. Try it on for size. See what results it produces. This is great fun! For example, suppose you want to be a self-made millionaire. Imagine yourself creating that result. What kind of person do you need to be in your mind (mentally, emotionally, and action-orientation-wise) to produce that result? Or imagine you want to be far more effective in your job. You want to achieve a real breakthrough. What kind of mindset do you need to produce that result? How do you need to set your mind to be a more effective parent or spouse?

To get into a particular mindset (e.g., the mindset needed to deliver an inspiring speech to 3,000 fellow professionals), you may simply have a single thought or mental image, or say a few words (e.g., I've got something really special to share with my fellow pros) and, bang, you're in it. For another mindset, you may have to write down a detailed description of how you have to be mentally, emotionally, and in action. You may need to develop really strong mental images of being that kind of person. And then mentally practice this success scenario, or practice it in front of a mirror or in the real world, before you get into it and make it your own.

In any case, it's helpful to understand that a powerful, productive mindset is a mental and emotional state that involves mental toughness, emotional control, and action orientation. To create useful mindsets, you need to capitalize on these three leverage points which you *can* control.

• *Mental toughness* is choosing what you want your mind to focus on—the result you want to produce—then locking on that result and staying locked on it until the result is produced.

Mental toughness also includes your total confidence that you can create that result.

• *Emotional control* is managing your emotional state so that it remains positive, resilient, and at the appropriate level of intensity, so that it helps produce the desired result rather than hinders it.

Research indicates that you are more likely to achieve your goal with minimal stress and wasted energy when your emotional state is *positive*. A negative emotional state is usually counterproductive at best and greatly increases stress, strain, and wasted energy. It seems that John-Roger and Peter Mc-Williams, authors of *You Can't Afford the Luxury of a Negative Thought*, are quite right. To help keep your emotional state positive for the rest of your life, join the Positive Thinkers Club; see Recommended Resources at end of chapter.

Emotional *resiliency* is the ability to recover quickly and bounce back when you encounter failure, setbacks, strong criticism, or personal injury.

The emotional *intensity* with which you produce desired results can be controlled and adjusted to the task at hand. Certain results may require a very intense, all-out effort; others may require only moderate or low-intensity effort. Sometimes it helps to monitor your intensity level on an imaginary intensity meter—like a speedometer—and consciously turn your intensity level up or down as needed.

The bottom line on emotional control is as follows: Pursue your desired results with a consistently positive and resilient emotional state but vary the intensity of your effort as required by the task at hand.

• *Action orientation* is always looking to see what action you can take to move closer to your goal and then taking that action. Not just any action. Not just busy work. But well-focused action that produces observable results. It's the ability to keep looking for, being open to, and generating possibilities that help you create your desired result, especially under adversity. It's being patient and persistent even when the odds are against you, or when everyone else is negative and has given up hope. Action orientation is looking at your ineffective effort not as a failure but as a learning experience that leads to an adjustment, another action, observation of the result, adjustment if necessary, another action, and so on, until the desired result is created. Action orientation is the ability to get yourself to take action, to do whatever needs to be done to successfully produce the result you desire.

By sharply focusing your mind on the result you want, by locking your mind on that target, and by controlling your emotional state regardless of the circumstances so that you stay focused on taking positive, constructive actions that produce that result, you make yourself nearly unstoppable. You have programmed yourself for success like a laser-guided missile that's locked on its target.

By being mentally and emotionally prepared, you don't let problems, pressures, setbacks, distractions, and disappointments bother you. You waste minimal time and energy dealing with these "stepping stones." You stay focused and channel your energy in productive ways to produce the results you desire.

Lack of mental focus, lack of emotional control, and lack of an action orientation render your mental powers useless and greatly diminish your personal effectiveness, your success, and the quality of your life.

You can be mentally tough every day by consciously choosing or creating the mindsets that will be most useful for you. Each morning, lock on the results you most want to produce in your job, family, and personal life, and lock on your guiding values. This is precisely what your Command and Control Center will help you do. Then, throughout the day choose from your collection of powerful, productive mindsets the ones that will be most helpful.

It's Your Choice

Make a deep-down choice right now about how you will use the awesome powers of your mind to create the results you desire most in life.

☐ 1. I can do almost anything if I put my mind to it. I choose to put my mind to it by consciously choosing powerful mindsets that help me produce the results I desire. I will be mentally tough, emotionally in control, and action oriented to create those results. I will focus my mind on creating those results, lock on them, and proceed with total confidence to create them with maximum velocity and joy and with minimum stress and wasted energy. I will remain positive and resilient at all times, regardless of the obstacles, opposition, and setbacks I may encounter, and vary my intensity according to the task at hand.

☐ 2. I can't do much of anything even if I try. I guess my mindset is basically negative and nonproductive. I choose to be mentally weak, emotionally out of control, and lazy when it comes to creating the results I want most. Actually, I really don't have any exciting dreams to pursue. Even if I did, I probably wouldn't put much effort into achieving them because I'd probably fail anyway. It's too much work. I get discouraged pretty easily. The world is basically against me. I just drift through life and see what happens to me. I really don't have any say. I have no power to do things differently.

Wise Supporting Actions

I certainly hope you locked on approach 1. Here are some specific actions that will make you mentally tough, emotionally in control, and action oriented. These wise actions will show you how to create and use powerful, productive mindsets before, during, and after events that are important to you.

Before a General Event, Consciously Choose a Mindset That Will Help Produce the Results You Desire in That Situation

For example, say the general event is *this day*. What kind of mindset will help you create the kind of day you desire? You might set your mind for the day by simply saying:

"I choose to create a terrific, fun-filled day by enjoying my work and my family, and by smiling at everyone I encounter and making them feel good about themselves by giving them a compliment!" or

"I choose to maintain a low-stress mindset at work. I choose to be cool, calm, collected, positive, productive and healthy at work today. And I will refocus my mind on this choice several times during the day to make it happen!"

Suppose the general event is the rest of your life. What kind of mindset will help you create the "rest of your life" you have in mind? If you have prepared your Command and Control Center, use that as a success scenario for the rest of your life. You can set your mind to produce that life by reading your desired life statement and your guiding values, then visualizing yourself living just like that. Imagine how powerful this would be if you took one minute or so every morning to do this. I highly recommend you make this a daily morning ritual.

A note about "being happy" as a way-of-life mindset: Happiness is a state of mind, a mindset. It comes from focusing on and *appreciating* what you have right now, at the present, instead of focusing on and being miserable about what you don't have. You can create an "I am happy" mindset at any time—it's just a matter of choosing it. This idea is so simple yet so hard for most people to comprehend.

For example, one evening a TV talk-show host was interviewing an elderly person who, as it turned out, stole the show with his upbeat attitude, humor, and genuine happiness. Everyone was roaring with laughter and having a great time. The host finally said to the guest, "You're quite a happy man, aren't you?" And the man said, "Of course I'm happy." "Well," said the host, "how did you get to be so happy?" And the old man said, "It's just as plain as the nose on your face. Every morning when you wake up you've got two choices—to be happy or to be unhappy. I've never been so dumb as to settle for unhappy."

Abe Lincoln said, "People are just about as happy as they make up their minds to be." Have you made up your mind to be happy or unhappy? You don't have to wait until you graduate from high school. You don't have to wait until you get your first car. You don't have to wait until you graduate from college. You don't have to wait until you get your first job. (Starting to sound familiar?) You don't have to wait until the project is finished. You don't have to wait until you get your next promotion. You don't have to wait until vacation time comes. You don't have to wait until the reorganization is over. You don't have to wait until you find another job. You don't have to wait until you retire. You can choose to be happy right now! It's a mindset. Go ahead. Try it right now. Say to yourself: "I've made up my mind. I choose to be happy right now and for the rest of my life! I *am* happy right now! I *can* feel it and I *love* the feeling!" (Smile!) If you are not ready to choose to be happy for the rest of your life, then start small and just choose to be happy for the next minute or the next hour.

Before a Specific Event, Consciously Choose a Mindset That Will Help Produce the Results You Desire in That Situation

Let's say you have been asked to give a presentation to the board of directors of your company. It's a situation that strikes fear in most people. But instead of asking "Why me?" develop a scenario and mindset for giving a successful presentation.

Your success scenario might be something like this: You enter the boardroom with a relaxed and friendly smile, standing tall, and feeling great about yourself. You feel the lush carpet beneath your feet. You see the gorgeous wood table and smell the fragrance of the beautiful floral centerpiece. You begin your presentation. (Describe exactly how you want your presentation to go. Notice what you say and how well you say it. Notice how poised and totally confident you are as you share your very interesting information with the board members.)

You are really hot. You can see the board members showing lots of interest. Your presentation is finished now, and board members come up to you and compliment you on an excellent presentation. You smile joyously and enjoy some friendly conversation before you exit and return to your office. What a fantastic presentation. On the way to your office, your broad smile remains and you bask in the warm glow of this pleasurable moment. You can't wait to tell everyone how well it went. You notice how powerful, self-confident, and in control you feel!

Champions are made in practice. Each day prior to the presentation, mentally rehearse this scenario. You can do this mental rehearsal wherever you can sit down, relax, close your eyes, and concentrate. You will be ready—a great success with much less stress.

I highly recommend you try this technique. It works! It has proven to be very effective in my own life and has produced dramatic results for my clients. It can be used for nearly any event, big or small, at work, at home, or anywhere. Here are the specifics of the procedure and a checklist that will help you.

This exciting procedure is based on the mental training techniques used by Olympic and other world-class athletes (see references to peak and optimal performance and to mental training techniques in Recommended Resources at the end of this chapter). You can use it any time you want to prepare yourself mentally for a specific event.

1. *Create a success scenario.* First, state precisely what result you desire to produce, by when, and how you are going to do it. Next, specify what mindset you need to produce that result in that way by that date. What kind of person do you need to be mentally, emotionally, and in action to make that happen? How will you feel when you've produced the result? Write these headings on a piece of paper and respond to them:

Desired result: _____

By when: _____

How—action plan: _____

Mentally, I need to be: _____

Emotionally, I need to be: _____

Action-wise, I need to be: _____

How I will feel when I've produced this result: _____

Now turn this information into a mental movie with you as the star. Visualize a clear and complete picture of yourself successfully doing what needs to be done to create the result you desire. Pay attention to how you are mentally and emotionally as well as to your actions. Enjoy the positive feelings that accompany your accomplishment. This is your success scenario—make it as real as possible. What do you see, hear, smell, taste? What colors? What movement? It's often helpful to develop your success scenario as a written script. Write it in the present tense as if you were doing it right now (I am . . .). This may take only a few minutes.

2. *Mentally rehearse your success scenario.* To program yourself for success:

* Get yourself into a state of deep relaxation.
* Mentally visualize your success scenario happening; be there (inside your body, not as an observer) doing exactly what needs to be done to achieve the desired result—really feel it, as if it were happening.
* Pay special attention to how you are mentally and emotionally. Are you focused, positive, emotionally in control, totally confident, at the appropriate level of intensity, powerful?
* Repeat the success scenario three times.

Repeat this mental rehearsal of your success scenario until you've really got your successful performance down pat (once a day, or several times a day for several days or several weeks). Repetition (practice, practice, practice) is essential in this programming technique. Ask any Olympic athlete! When the time comes to perform and the pressure is on, you are ready and totally confident. After all, you've done it successfully, many, many times in your mind as well as in practice (remember, this is your mental training, it doesn't replace your real-world practice). You have literally programmed yourself for success.

You can use the following checklist to make sure all your mental and emotional systems are go.

Checklist for Creating a Powerful, Productive Mindset

Mental toughness or focus:

☐ My mind is focused on the target. I tell my mind exactly what result I want to produce, how I am going to produce it, what kind of person I need to be (mentally, emotionally, and action-wise) to produce it, and how I will feel when I've produced it. This is my success scenario.

☐ I am locked on my target.

☐ I am totally confident that I can create this result. This strong belief is the source of my power.

☐ I commit to producing this result by such and such time or date. Consider it done. I have killed off any known obstacles, excuses, or whatever else could distract me.

Emotional control:

☐ I am in a positive emotional state.

☐ I am at the appropriate level of intensity.

☐ I am emotionally resilient. If I should encounter a setback, strong criticism, or frustration, I will recover quickly, stay positive and confident, and bounce back, continuing toward my target.

Action orientation:

☐ I mentally rehearse my success scenario.

☐ I take well-focused action that moves me closer to my target with the efficiency and velocity of a laser beam. But I don't wait forever to take the perfect action. I'm willing to take action, produce a result, learn from it, make an adjustment, and take the next action. I don't waste my energy or time on actions I know won't move me closer to my desired result.

☐ I don't see failures as failures but as ineffective actions, learning experiences, and great opportunities for mid-course corrections. I use both effective and ineffective actions to enhance the positive momentum toward my target.

☐ I stay alert and open to discovering possible actions that will help move me closer to my desired result.

During an Event, Consciously Choose a Mindset That Will Help Produce the Results You Desire During This Event

This is live, in-the-present moment programming of your mind and it only takes a few seconds. For example, suppose you are at a boring party or endless meeting that you can't just leave. As soon as you realize that you have a "this is really boring" mindset, recognize it as a take charge point—a chance to choose a mindset that will serve you better in this situation. You have an opportunity to look at this event as fun—as a personal challenge, a chance to experiment with interpersonal skills, to practice listening with empathy and establishing rapport with people you don't much like. It is a chance to practice centering yourself and dealing with individuals in calm openness and with genuine love. Instead of sticking with your negative "this is really boring" mindset and making yourself miserable, you consciously change to a "this is really fun" mindset and look for the good that's waiting to be discovered. You go after it and enjoy the process.

After an Unwanted Event, Consciously Choose a Mindset That Will Produce the Results You Desire as You Respond to What Happened to You

This is extremely valuable. Pay close attention.

What do you do when something bad happens or when things don't go the way you want? What do you do when you experience a major setback or disappointment? Try consciously choosing a mindset that will do you some good. For example:

• Remember that bad stuff happens to everyone, even to good people like you. (Remember we all have problems and we will always have problems.) So it's not what happens to you in life that matters, but how you respond to what happens! You can handle any situation effectively, if you choose to.

• Acknowledge what happened and tell yourself the truth about it. Don't deny that what happened, happened.

• Acknowledge your negative feelings and express them (this hurts, I'm angry, it feels like my heart's been ripped out, it's depressing). This is normal, healthy, and necessary. The length of time it takes to move through this step can vary from a one-minute "pity party" to several months of grieving, depending on the situation. *The key is to pass through it as fast as possible and not get stuck in it.*

• Acknowledge that what happened is over now and it's past history. Learn whatever lessons are to be learned, then let go of this unwanted event; let go of your negative emotions.

• Demonstrate your resilience. The unwanted event *could* really get you down and set you back, but don't let it! Consciously choose a positive, empowering mindset and take action. Is there a way to look at this event that will empower you? Is it a stepping stone on the way to success? Is it a valuable (albeit painful) learning experience? Can you respond to it in a way that will make you healthier, happier, and more effective? Choose a new desired result you now want to create with respect to this event. You may still want the result you originally desired. You may want to modify your original desire or want something different now. Whatever your new desire, focus on it and take action that supports your choice. (The checklist for creating a powerful, productive mindset will help launch you.)

Let's say you gave that presentation to the board of directors and it did not go well. Instead of coming back to your office lamenting how bad it was and going through umpteen verses of "gee, ain't it awful" (eventually this conversation with yourself gets down to "gee, ain't I awful" and, zip, there goes your self-esteem). Instead of spinning your wheels in the mud of self-pity and wasting all that precious time and energy, instead of doing all that nonproductive, unhealthy stuff, try something like this. Say:

That presentation did not go as I had planned. I took an action and produced a result. A poor presentation—an unwanted result. How can I look at this experience in a way that empowers me? What's something positive I can learn from this experience [no need to label it as a failure]? [Answer the questions.] Good. Now, is this an area in which I want to produce a better result next time? If so, what will I do differently next time? [Take a minute to focus your mind on the result you intend to produce the next time and consciously commit to doing exactly that.] Next time I definitely will give an excellent presentation, and I will use my mental toughness, emotional control, and action orientation to create that result. Period. Amen. Conversation is over.

Move on to another activity. There, you just saved yourself a tremendous amount of energy—energy that is normally wasted on extended pity parties. After experiencing a major setback or disappointment, some people spend days, weeks, months, or even years spinning their wheels in that mud of self-pity. What a waste of energy and time.

You have preserved your energy and have taken good care of yourself. You have used your mental toughness, emotional resilience, and action orientation. You have taken this unwanted event in stride and have energy to channel into some other productive activity.

You can call this the "refocus-on-what-you-want-and-don't-waste-time-and-energy-wallowing-in-the-mud-of-self-pity" technique.

Start a Collection of Powerful, Productive Mindsets

Collect mindsets that you personally find effective at producing desired results. You might keep these on 3 × 5 cards, on a page in your "time manager," or, later on, in your Personal Effectiveness Plan.

Your guiding values are no doubt excellent mindsets (that's why they are in your Command and Control Center). Jot down other useful, empowering mindsets that come to mind right now:

1. _____
2. _____
3. _____
4. _____

You might also make a list of mindsets that you have found to be not useful.

1. _____
2. _____
3. _____
4. _____

Here are some mindsets I have found empowering. See if any of these might make you more effective, healthier, and happier.

Yes I can! Assume no limitations. Just do it.
I can make a profound difference in people's lives.
I approach problems in a cool, calm, confident manner.
I can create the life I truly want by making choices and
    taking action.
Nothing's going to stop me. Consider it done.
Attack! (the ski slope, the problem, the challenge, but not
    people)
I'll be gentle.
It ain't over till it's over.
I do my best and let God do the rest.
If I did know what to do, it would probably be something
    like. . . .
Strong mental images of the result I desire really help me
    produce that result.
I'm 100 percent responsible for me and my health, effec-
    tiveness, and happiness.
Ask for help.
I don't waste time and energy on negative emotions.

The real issue is. . . . What's missing is. . . .
The best way to get on my feet is to get off my ass.
I feel calm, centered, and in control as I go through each day.
I refuse to let problems or frustrations interfere with my success, health, and happiness.
I choose to look for the good in everyone and everything.
What's important about sidewalks is you can walk on them. What's important about . . . is. . . .
People who feel good about themselves produce good results.
There's nothing that can scare me. I have no fear.
I will make people shine.
I can handle anything.
I don't have to be perfect. I'm not perfect but parts of me are excellent.
I will make a game out of this.

And here is a list of some mindsets I have found to be disempowering:

It can't be done.
I can't do this. I can't handle this.
I have to be perfect. It has to be perfect.
I don't like to do things I don't do well.
I woulda, coulda, shoulda.
It's black or white, either this or that.

You Can Do Almost Anything If You Put Your Mind to It!

Make sure the incredible powers of your mind are working *for* you, not against you. Choose the results you want and choose the mindsets that will help you create those results with speed and with minimal stress.

Caution: Don't be so focused on producing a singular result that other parts of your life get out of balance and eventually undermine your effectiveness, health, and happiness.

Be aware that your mental and emotional toughness can be perceived as insensitivity to the needs of others, especially to their emotional needs. Incorporate into your mental and emotional toughness an ability to deal effectively with people who may be less focused or less mentally and emotionally tough than you.

Recommended Resources

Garfield, Charles. *Peak Performance: Mental Training Techniques of the World's Greatest Athletes*. New York: Warner Books, 1984.

Graham Scott, Gini. *Mind Power: Picture Your Way to Success in Business*. Englewood Cliffs, N.J.: Prentice-Hall, 1987. Also available in a 4-cassette and 32-page workbook package titled *Mind Power: Visualizing Your Success in Business*. Englewood Cliffs, N.J.: Prentice-Hall, 1989.

Loehr, James, and Peter McLaughlin. *Mentally Tough: The Principles of Winning at Sports Applied to Winning in Business*. New York: M. Evans and Co., 1986.

Miller, Emmett. *Optimal Performance*. Audiocassette. Stanford, Calif.: Source Cassette Learning System, 1983.

———. *Power Vision: Life Mastery Through Mental Imagery*. Audiocassette. Chicago: Nightingale-Conant, 1987.

———. *Writing Your Own Script*. Audiocassette. Stanford, Calif.: Source Cassette Learning System, 1980.

Suinn, Richard. *Seven Steps to Peak Performance: The Mental Training Manual for Athletes*. Toronto: Hans Huber Publishers, 1986.

For more information about the Positive Thinkers Club, write to the Foundation for Christian Living, P.O. Box FCL, Pawling, New York 12564.

I CHOOSE TO BE
MENTALLY TOUGH,
EMOTIONALLY IN CONTROL,
AND ACTION ORIENTED EVERY DAY.

```
.........
:  ___  :
: | 11 | :
: |___| :
:.........:
```

Choose to Communicate in a Positive, Productive, Low-Stress Manner

"The way we communicate with others and the way we communicate with ourselves ultimately determine the quality of our lives."

—Anthony Robbins, Unlimited Power

If you want to use your conversations with people to help produce the results you desire, or if you want to be cool, calm, and collected in pressure-packed situations, then choose to communicate with people in a positive, productive, low-stress manner. This is Daily Power Choice 6.

How It Works

When you talk with people you have either a positive or a negative effect on them. Based on your communication style, they either want to be with you more and cooperate with you or not want to be with you and not want to cooperate with you. It's important for you to be aware of this all the time, especially when you are dealing with a difficult problem or a stressful situation.

You can tell what effect you've had on people by looking at their reactions to you. If it was a punishing experience (negative, stressful, nonproductive for them, lowered their self-esteem), they will interact with you as little as possible. They will want to avoid you. If it was a rewarding experience for them (positive, productive, low-stress, empowered them, en-

142

hanced their self-esteem), they will want to interact with you more.

Like smiling, low-stress communication seems a common-sense thing to do, but many executives, managers, and professionals seem oblivious to the idea. Positive, low-stress communication is not in their repertoire. Some, perhaps, can do it under normal conditions but not when the pressure is on.

This Daily Power Choice empowers you to converse with people in a positive, productive, low-stress way that helps you produce the results you desire and keeps the stress level at a minimum. (The concept of low-stress communication is based on Karl Albrecht's *Stress and the Manager*.)

Granted, there are situations where it may be impossible to have a positive, constructive, low-stress conversation. However, it is certainly in your own best interest to make as many of your conversations as you can positive, constructive, and low-stressed for the other person. You can use this style of communication anywhere—at work, at home, on the phone, at the store.

It's Your Choice

Make a deep-down choice right now about how you want to communicate with people for the rest of your life.

- ☐ 1. I choose to communicate with people in a positive, productive, low-stress manner that enhances their self-esteem, gains their cooperation, and makes for enjoyable, rewarding interactions.
- ☐ 2. I choose to communicate with people in a negative, nonproductive, high-stress manner that puts people down, makes them not want to cooperate, and makes for miserable, punishing interactions.

Wise Supporting Actions

I'm sure you chose option 1. Here are some specifics actions that will help you communicate with people in a positive, productive, low-stress manner.

Check Yourself Out

Ask yourself to what extent people take the initiative in contacting and communicating with you, in sharing ideas and viewpoints with you, and in including you in their personal and social activities. Your answers indicate whether your manner of communicating is primarily punishing or rewarding for others.

Use More Rewarding and Fewer Punishing Behaviors in Your Conversations

Do you use primarily rewarding or punishing behaviors in your conversations? Here is a checklist you can use to examine the nature of your conversations (adapted from Karl Albrecht, *Stress and the Manager*). To make yourself more effective, use more rewarding behaviors in your conversations and fewer punishing behaviors.

Checklist for Taking Charge of Your Conversations

Rewarding, stress-reducing, emotionally satisfying behaviors:

- ☐ Treating the other person with respect and dignity throughout the entire conversation
- ☐ Giving others a chance to express views or share information
- ☐ Maintaining or enhancing their self-esteem
- ☐ Listening attentively, hearing them out, not interrupting
- ☐ Being totally present with the person; no distractions
- ☐ Sharing information, opinions, and one's self with others
- ☐ Smiling, greeting positively
- ☐ Using nonverbal gestures of acceptance and respect
- ☐ Seeking first to understand and then to be understood (purposefully listen to understand what they are saying and feeling, and withhold your tendency to judge, evaluate, approve, or disapprove immediately)

- [ ] Praising and complimenting others sincerely
- [ ] Compromising, negotiating, helping others succeed
- [ ] Talking positively and constructively
- [ ] Acknowledging the feelings and needs of others
- [ ] Stating one's needs and desires honestly
- [ ] Delaying your "automatic" emotional reactions; not flying off the handle
- [ ] Leveling with people without leveling them
- [ ] Confronting others constructively on difficult issues
- [ ] Expressing genuine interest in the other person
- [ ] Consciously striving for a win-win relationship
- [ ] Having a positive, constructive orientation during the conversation
- [ ] Acknowledging the feelings of others and responding with empathy
- [ ] Giving suggestions constructively
- [ ] Stating agreement with others when possible, telling them they are right
- [ ] Telling people they are important, special, appreciated
- [ ] Restating other people's ideas and feelings so that they know you heard and understood them
- [ ] Enjoying good humor
- [ ] Attacking the problem, not the person
- [ ] Keeping confidential conversations confidential
- [ ] Being joyful and enthusiastic in your conversations with others

Punishing, stress-producing, emotionally dissatisfying behaviors:

- [ ] Yelling, screaming
- [ ] Monopolizing the conversation
- [ ] Interrupting others, not hearing them out
- [ ] Verbally attacking and abusing others
- [ ] Putting down, insulting, embarrassing, belittling, or otherwise lowering their self-esteem
- [ ] Complaining or whining excessively
- [ ] Losing your temper
- [ ] Not being straight with people, telling lies or not saying everything

☐ Pushing others with words; overusing "shoulds"
☐ Insincere flattery
☐ Bragging, talking only about self
☐ Negative, destructive orientation
☐ Not listening attentively, not being totally present with the person, allowing yourself to be distracted
☐ Using nonverbal gestures of disrespect
☐ Criticizing excessively, fault finding
☐ Demanding one's own way, refusing to negotiate or compromise
☐ Being sour faced or stern; not smiling
☐ Ignoring people; withholding customary social behaviors such as friendly greetings, eye contact, "uh-huhs", nods, etc.
☐ Not respecting other people's right to have their own opinion
☐ Making others feel guilty
☐ Losing your temper easily
☐ Playing "games" with people
☐ Not answering honest questions
☐ Not leveling with people
☐ Not saying what you mean, not meaning what you say
☐ Not being thorough or complete in your conversation, forgetting to include a piece of important information (who, what, when, where)
☐ Disagreeing routinely
☐ Not allowing any freedom
☐ Not doing what you say you will do, not following through on agreement, promises, or commitments
☐ Violating confidentiality
☐ Saying, "Yes, but. . . ."

Be Gracious

Practice putting others at ease and help them stay that way through the entire conversation, especially in stressful situations. Many people who rise to the top in their profession are gracious, polite, and courteous. They can make anyone feel important, respected, and at ease.

Be Aware of Factors That Have a Negative Impact on Your Ability to Communicate in a Positive, Productive, Low-Stress Way

Fatigue, stress, lack of time (because of deadlines or your own unwarranted sense of urgency), hunger, or low blood sugar can make it difficult to communicate in an effective manner. Recognize when this happens and take appropriate action. For example, eat frequently enough to keep your blood-sugar level up. If you are too stressed or too tired to have an effective conversation, reschedule it for when you will feel less stressed or are reenergized.

Take the Time to Communicate Effectively

You may think that you are a very busy person with lots to do and so little time to do it. Positive, productive communication that will really help you create the results you desire requires time—sometimes just a little time and sometimes a lot of time. Make the time. You'll be very glad you did!

For example, take the extra one or two minutes to give someone clear, complete instructions. Pay attention to details. Don't assume the other person knows what to do or how to do it. And give some understanding and encouragement. Boost his or her self-esteem with a compliment.

Actively Manage Your Conversation So That It Produces the Result You Desire

Take 100 percent responsibility for ensuring your message is received and understood. Manage the conversation. This means taking charge of your speaking and listening, as well as managing their listening.

First, know what your objective is. Do you want the person to understand something? To be aware of something? To take some action? Get the person's attention. Make sure he or she is listening to you. Many people talk without ever getting the other person's attention. This happens a lot, for example, between family members.

In difficult situations, keep your objective in mind and stay focused on achieving that result in a positive, constructive, low-stress manner. Be careful not to get sidetracked. If you find yourself sidetracked, refocus immediately on your objective and get back on track.

If you are asking someone to do something important, say that it is important. Give all the details (who, what, where, when, why, how) needed to take successful action. Check for understanding, don't assume it. And ask, "Is there anything else you need to know?" Get the person's agreement on the course of action and ask for a commitment: "Can I count on you to get this done by Tuesday?

Also, take 100 percent responsibility for how you come across. If you want to come across as cool, calm, and collected, then speak in a cool, calm, and collected way and check to see if you are coming across that way. Monitor yourself and observe the other person's reactions. If you're not sure, ask, "How am I coming across to you?" Or, if it's obvious you are not coming across the way you want, say so and make adjustments. Don't blame others for how you come across to them; that's your responsibility.

Take Your Status or Power Level Into Account

Parents, bosses, doctors, lawyers, and other authority figures usually don't realize how powerful they appear to others. If you are in a position of power, every word you say, how you say it, every gesture can be given undue importance or be completely distorted. And because people are intimidated and fearful, they may be reluctant to ask for clarification or share information with you. Consequently, it's not easy for the people "at the top" to get the full story. You need to take the initiative to build positive, productive, rewarding (in their eyes) relationships with people. Put them at ease. Act like a normal human being, not an overbearing authority figure. Use the rewarding behaviors in your conversations.

Have Positive, Productive, Low-Stress Conversations With Yourself

Treat yourself with respect and dignity. Don't talk in a negative, nonconstructive, stressful way to yourself. If you are distressed about something in your life, have a positive, productive, low-stress conversation with yourself. Don't bad-mouth yourself. Use the rewarding behaviors with yourself.

Seek to understand yourself, and ask yourself empowering questions whenever you feel down. For example, you might ask yourself: "What's going on? What's working? What's not working? What am I assuming? What's missing? What are possible solutions? What wise choices can I make? What wise actions can I take?"

Make Positive, Productive, Low-Stress Conversations a Way of Life

Make it a habit to have positive, productive, low-stress conversations with people. You may want to make this one of your guiding values. The rewards for both you and others are enormous. Just imagine the possibilities when you consistently have positive, productive, low-stress conversations with everyone you encounter. In short, your personal effectiveness, health, and quality of life are directly related to the quality of your conversations with people (and with yourself).

Recommended Resources

Albrecht, Karl. *Stress and the Manager*. New York: Simon & Schuster, 1979.

```
I CHOOSE TO COMMUNICATE
IN A POSITIVE,
PRODUCTIVE,
LOW-STRESS MANNER EVERY DAY.
```

Choose to Be Spiritually Strong, Resilient, and Joyful Every Day

"May THE FORCE be with you."

If you want to go through life totally confident that you can deal with anything that comes your way, if you've reached the top and have it all, but feel empty and are now wondering, "Is that all there is?" . . . If you are struggling with a really tough situation, or if you've reached bottom and your situation seems hopeless. . . .

You can be in control of your life but realize that in an instant, something catastrophic could happen that reminds you people can never be in *total* control—that there is a greater force, a force that can blow away all the extraneous aspects of your life and realign your priorities instantly. You can sense there is something else you need to quell your underlying uneasiness, to put you at peace.

If you are awestruck by a baby's warm tiny hand wrapped around one of your fingers, by the metamorphosis of a caterpillar into a butterfly, by the order of the universe, and wonder, "Where did all this come from? What's the source?" If you sense that there is something else you need to quell your underlying uneasiness, to put you at peace, then choose to nourish, strengthen, and make full use of your spiritual power every day. This is Daily Power Choice 7.

This chapter gets to the core of our lives. It deals with a very personal matter—your spiritual power—without reference to any particular philosophy or religion. For present purposes, I'll refer to this invisible and indescribable spiritual power simply as your Higher Power. You may refer to it as God, Allah, Yahweh, Tao, Brahma, Buddha, or your maker, the source, universal love, the power of the universe, the creator, the lifeforce, a higher level of consciousness, Mother Nature, your innermost self, the ultimate reality, the supernatural being, the light, or the big force behind it all. That's fine. Whatever that force is, that's what I'm talking about. Feel free to replace my label with your label. What's important is that you recognize the existence of this powerful force and make use of it.

How It Works

"We are not human beings having a spiritual experience. We are spiritual beings having a human experience."

—*Teilhard de Chardin*

Your spiritual power is one of the three components (body, mind, spirit) of your personal effectiveness. Your spirit is your very essence—the real you. It is that fascinating, unchanging part of you, separate from your body, that is watching you read this book. It is the powerful essence deep within you that seems bigger than life itself, that connects you with a level of power, wisdom, love, and peace that exists far beyond your assumed limitations. It is this indescribable spiritual force that makes you far greater, far more powerful than you think are.

I don't pretend to know how it works, but I'll share with you some things that I've learned to date. It seems you have access to your Higher Power if you choose to access it. This Daily Power Choice is about consciously choosing, in your own heart and in your own way, to relate to, align with, and make full use of your awesome spiritual power every day.

If you can conceive of the possibility that there might be a Higher Power. If you can truly believe that there really is a Higher Power, then you can gain access to this greater power. The key is simply to believe in it. As Dr. Wayne Dyer (author of *The Awakened Life*) says you must believe it before you can see it. And the key to making full use of this powerful force is simply your willingness to make use of it.

"I could not say I believe. I know! I have had the experience of being gripped by something that is stronger than myself, something that people call God."

—*Carl Jung*

As a believer in your Higher Power, you can develop very powerful spiritual tools like a positive, upbeat outlook on life; a meaningful purpose in life, a sense of where you fit into the universe; the enduring values of love, hope, charity, forgiveness, trust, acceptance; other guidelines for relating to yourself and to other people. These tools, if used, help you replace fear and worry with confidence and inner peace and really help you maximize your contribution to and enjoyment of life. By believing in your Higher Power, you have an opportunity to look at and respond to the world in a new way. You have an opportunity to go through life feeling very calm, centered, totally loved, peaceful, joyous, and confident that you have all the strength and power you need to meet any challenge that comes your way. You have genuine hope of a better life—an eternal life, and a secure feeling that your "better future" is guaranteed—*a total sense of security*.

So to make full use of your spiritual power, you consciously choose to believe there is a Higher Power that you have access to, and you consciously choose to use this power in your life. Note how this exemplifies the making choices and taking action approach to life described in this book. And how, without the action, the belief is meaningless.

Spiritual nutrition and activity strengthen your spirit and make you feel very special, and thus have a strong positive effect on your mental attitude, self-esteem, health, and behavior. The stronger your spirit, the more energy and resilience you have, and the more you can use your talents in a cool, calm, collected, positive, productive, and joyful way. Spiritual strength is a key factor in improving the quality of your life.

You can nourish, strengthen, and use your spiritual power

at any time: when you wake up, during the day, or when you go to bed; when you are really enjoying life and when you are really struggling.

You can call upon your spiritual power when you are suffering from an inescapable addiction. In fact, the program that has proved to have dramatic, long-term success in helping people conquer addictions is the twelve-step AA-type program that includes recognizing and accepting the existence of a Higher Power, asking that Higher Power for help, trusting the Higher Power to help, and forgiving yourself and others.

You can also call upon your spiritual power when you come to a crossroads in your life. That's what Tom Monaghan, CEO of Domino's Pizza, did. As a young boy, he was placed in an orphanage and foster homes. He started with nothing and built the number-one pizza delivery business and amassed a fortune of over $500 million. Then, he reached a crossroads (a take charge point) in his life. In a 1989 interview for *USA Today*, he said, "Accumulating and accumulating [300 classic cars, $30 million art collection, Detroit Tigers baseball team, etc.], that's all I've been doing for the last 30 years, and what the heck for?" After getting all the material things he had ever dreamed of, he said, "The great lesson of that is it's not that big a deal." He decided to take some actions that would get him more involved in what he called the Main Event: doing God's work. And he has proceeded to do so.

It's Your Choice

Make a deep-down choice right now about what kind of spiritual condition you want to be in for the rest of your life.

☐ 1. I choose to go through life spiritually strong, resilient, and joyful. I choose to take full advantage of the spirit, the energy, the joy, the love, the peace, and the wisdom available to me through my strong belief and trust in a Higher Power.

☐ 2. I choose to neglect this third component of my personal effectiveness. I choose to go through life spiritually weak, more vulnerable to stress and strain, and without true inner peace and confidence.

I hope you chose option 1. If so, take this little quiz to get an idea of how clear and strong your belief in your Higher Power really is.

1. What are your beliefs about this Higher Power? (Not your religion's beliefs but *your* beliefs.)
2. How strong are your beliefs? How strong is your spiritual muscle?
3. How does your daily life reflect these beliefs? Are you taking action that supports your beliefs? Are you living your beliefs regardless of obstacles, opposition, circumstances?
4. Are you willing to take a stand for your spiritual beliefs?

Wise Supporting Actions

Here are some specific actions that will help you nourish, strengthen, make use of, and enjoy your spiritual power.

Experience Your Spirituality—Your Higher Power

"My religion consists of a humble admiration of the illimitable superior spirit who reveals himself in the slight details we are able to perceive with our frail and feeble minds."

—Albert Einstein

This Higher Power seems to be revealed in unlimited ways. Spiritual experiences can be quite varied and unique. From now on, however and whenever you experience this spiritual power, tune in to it just a little bit more. Increase your awareness of the spiritual power *within* you—not merely intellectually, but emotionally and experientially. Open yourself up to its presence. Allow yourself to be touched by this force. Know in your heart that the force is real.

Feel it when you read a beautiful poem. Sense it when you admire an incredible painting or a joyful piece of music. Savor the feeling.

Increase your awareness of this Higher Power *outside* of you, in your environment, in other people, in nature, in the world, in the universe. Know it's present when you observe a soldier returning home to the outstretched arms of his loved ones. Notice how you feel when you gaze at the countless bright shining stars on a crystal-clear night. Notice how you feel when you really connect with another human (and spiritual) being. Think about the mind-boggling miracles all around you that you take for granted daily. Like the creation and development of a human life, the air, water, and soil, a sunrise or a sunset, the diversity of plants and animals, daytime and nighttime, your own high-tech body, and you as a one-of-a-kind creation of this universe!

Your environment can greatly facilitate your awareness of your Higher Power's presence. For some people this spiritual force seems most real, most present when they are in a quiet place and their body and mind are still. That's when they can hear that quiet, small voice. That quiet, sacred place can be in their home, at church, in the woods, at the shore, or anywhere. For other people, the Higher Power seems most real in the excitement of a frantic moment—making their way through whitewater rapids, skiing an expert slope, or saving a child in a blazing house, for instance. For yet other people the spiritual force seems most present in activities and places somewhere in between these two extremes. The possibilities are limitless.

Wherever and however this Higher Power seems most real to you, experience it more fully. Be strengthened and revitalized by it. And start noticing where else in your life this spiritual feeling starts showing up.

And practice living in the presence of your Higher Power. You will find yourself to be a different person. You will be transformed, empowered. Simply believe strongly that your Higher Power is always present. Feel it, enjoy it, be comforted by it. At any hour of the day or night, regardless of the circumstances or of what else is going on, your Higher Power is always with you.

Learn More About Your Spiritual Power

Most of us are on the low end of the scale when it comes to spiritual literacy. Just as there are many ways to experience the presence of your Higher Power, there are many ways to learn more about your spiritual power.

Observe and talk to other people. Learn from them in a nonjudgmental way and share your spiritual experiences with them; most people are eager to do this, but often assume that most other people aren't. Your learning will be enhanced if you respect the fact that human beings explore and express their spirituality in a wide variety of ways, and if you are careful not to force your particular way onto someone else.

In this day of global corporations and global competition, your coworker or customer may have spiritual beliefs quite different from your own, and these beliefs may have a strong impact on how that person lives his or her life and conducts business. From a purely business point of view, it makes good sense to be spiritually literate with respect to your own and other people's beliefs and practices. Check your library for *The Sacred Writings of the World's Great Religions* by S. E. Frost, Jr. It provides an excellent capsule summary of the thirteen great religions of the world, their basic beliefs, their sacred writings, their numbers of followers. It also has an excellent section that compares what the different religions have to say about key topics such as love, anger, meditation, sin, future life, happiness, work, the golden rule, etc. The similiarities are amazing!

Listen to radio broadcasts and audiotape programs, and read the spiritual literature from a variety of sources to learn more about your Higher Power (see Recommended Resources).

Note: I believe your first priority is to develop a personal, one-on-one relationship with your Higher Power. You should come to truly know your Higher Power through your own life experiences. Then, if you so desire, seek to enhance your personal relationship with your Higher Power by joining with others in an organized approach to spiritual development, realizing full well that religious organizations are human organizations and humans are not perfect in all that they do. Humans can screw up religious organizations just as well as they can screw up any other kind of organization.

We know that religious organizations can, indeed, turn us off and stifle our spiritual development. We also know that religious organizations can skyrocket our spiritual development and enjoyment of life, and help us through difficult times. If the religious organization you belong to isn't contributing to your spiritual fulfillment, either take action that will improve its ability to do so or initiate a search to find one that does (see Harold Kushner's *Who Needs God*, in Recommended Resources at end of chapter). In any event, don't let a bad experience with an imperfect human religious organization prevent you from developing a strong, personal relationship with your Higher Power right now.

Make Full Use of Your Spiritual Power Daily

Consciously align with your Higher Power on a daily basis. Do it first thing in the morning or the last thing at night. Any time is fine. Just do it.

You might read a passage from the Bible and reflect on it. You might read a short, one-minute spiritual message such as can be found in *Daily Power Thoughts*, by Dr. Robert Schuller. You might review your guiding values in your Command and Control Center.

Or develop the spirit-raising habit of having a daily quiet time that you spend with your Higher Power. Have a joyful conversation or say a favorite prayer. Prayer is simply talking to your Higher Power. Beware of rote prayer; if you are just saying words with no real meaning and feeling, then it is better to talk in your own words.

Let your Higher Power be your best friend and adviser— your partner at work, your partner at home, your partner for life, through good times and bad. Seek the advice and help of your Higher Power any time. Just quiet your mind and ask about your mission in life. Ask for guidance and support in fulfilling your mission. Use this tremendous creative, healing, loving force.

Your Higher Power can be your greatest confidence

builder! Keep comforting and inspiring words in front of you. When you feel overwhelmed, stressed out, lonely, depressed, discouraged, or confused, you are forgetting about your Higher Power. Reestablish contact with your Higher Power, and you will discover that a new peaceful state will interrupt your stress reaction so you can realize that your Higher Power watches over you and guides you, and that you can trust and depend on this Higher Power.

Add Your Spiritual Power to Your Daily Power Choices

You can strength the Daily Power Choices by putting your Higher Power behind them. For example:

- Daily Power Choice 1: Use this instant relaxation response: "Relax. My Higher Power and I can handle this effectively."
- Daily Power Choice 2: Take rest and relaxation breaks with your Higher Power. You can also add spiritual power to your deep breathing technique by breathing in the love, peace, and serenity of your Higher Power as you inhale and breathing out your stress as your exhale.
- Daily Power Choice 3: Meditate on and center your mind on love, beauty, peace, serenity, or other calming spiritual experiences (see Gerald Jampolsky and Diane Cirincione's *The Quiet Mind* and Herbert Benson's *Beyond the Relaxation Response* in Recommended Resources at end of chapter).
- Daily Power Choice 4: Let your Higher Power accompany you on your daily walk or run or other exercise. Express thanks for the good health you enjoy. Exercise your attitude of gratitude.
- Daily Power Choice 5: Ask your Higher Power to guide and support you as you set your goals and program yourself for success, health, and happiness.
- Daily Power Choice 6: Communicate with everyone in a manner that clearly indicates you love and respect them.

Add Love to Everything You Do

Love is a key element of your spiritual power. Think love, feel love, act lovingly. Picture your love flowing out to touch the lives of others.

The unlimited supply of love energy is one of the best things about being spiritually strong. You can give love to everyone and everything and your supply of love never diminishes. And when you give love you get love. This ability to give love to everything you do and to everyone you meet (including yourself) is one thing that can really create an enormous breakthrough—a quantum leap—in the quality of your life.

Love is a healing force and a creative force. You can see it working right before your eyes. Love may, indeed, conquer all. Love may be what the spiritual life is all about. It is the spiritual nutrition we need to do our personal best. Notice how your body, mind, and spirit feel when you feel "not loved." And notice how your body, mind, and spirit feel when you feel loved.

We all need love. It's essential. There are billions of people on this planet. They all need love. Talk about a great opportunity. Go for it! But start with yourself and your family. And then your boss, subordinates, coworkers, neighbors, and community members.

When Dr. Norman Vincent Peale, who wrote *The Power of Positive Thinking*, was asked what he would most like to be remembered for, he said: "I want to be remembered for loving people—all kinds of people. And for believing in their potential." Open yourself to unlimited love. Make your whole life an expression of love!

Forgive Someone

Forgiveness is a key element of spiritual strength. The act of forgiveness is very powerful. It can completely transform both the forgiver and the forgiven, giving new life, new energy, new possibilities. Be willing to forgive people who have done something to interfere with the positive, loving relationship you want to have with them. Love is for giving, and love is forgiving. Forgiveness sets you free. You can hate the sin and get angry at the sin, but love the sinner (see *The Quiet Mind* in Recommended Resources at end of chapter).

And if you don't have a positive, loving relationship with yourself, be willing to forgive yourself totally of whatever made it that way. This is one of the most important things you can do for yourself. Love is forgiving yourself when you need to.

Trust Your Higher Power

Another key element of spiritual strength is trust, especially when it seems your Higher Power is not looking out for you or when you are going through a painful experience. If you are spiritually strong and resilient, you can act with total confidence and trust in your Higher Power. It's an act of faith. You do your best and let your Higher Power do the rest.

As Tom Crum says in his book *The Magic of Conflict*, "You let go and let God. Letting go is never easy when we are holding on to something we consider precious. And yet, often it is exactly what we need to do." He tells this story: "There was a man hanging from a cliff two thousand feet above the valley floor. The terrified man looked to the top of the cliff and screamed, 'Is there anyone up there who can help me?' A deep, booming reply came from above, 'Yes, I'll help you. I'm the Lord. Just relax and let go.' A long pause. 'Is there anybody else up there who can help me?' "

A strong belief and trust in your Higher Power can get you through anything. Genuine peace of mind, body, and soul come from trusting your Higher Power. If you can't trust your Higher Power, whom can you trust?

Recommended Resources

Benson, Herbert. *Beyond the Relaxation Response*. New York: Times Books, 1984.
Dyer, Wayne. *The Awakened Life: Beyond Success, Achievement, and Performance*. Six audiocassettes. Chicago: Nightingale-Conant Corp., 1990.

Frost, S. E., Jr. *The Sacred Writings of the World's Great Religions.* New York: McGraw-Hill, 1972.

Jampolsky, Gerald, and Diane Cirincione. *The Quiet Mind: Imagery for Peaceful Living.* Six audiocassettes. Chicago: Nightingale-Conant Corp.

Kushner, Harold. *Who Needs God.* New York: Pocket Books, 1989.

Peale, Norman Vincent. *The Power of Positive Thinking.* Englewood Cliffs, N.J.: Prentice-Hall, 1978.

————. *The Power of Positive Thinking.* Six audiocassettes. Chicago: Nightingale-Conant Corp., 1988.

Pearce, Bill. "Nightsounds." A radio program. It provides a peaceful opportunity for spiritual reflection and centering. To learn which stations carry the program in your area, write Nightsounds, Box 29, Wheaton, IL, 60189.

Schuller, Robert. *Daily Power Thoughts.* New York: Jove Publications, 1983.

I CHOOSE TO BE
SPIRITUALLY STRONG,
RESILIENT,
AND JOYFUL EVERY DAY.

13

Fun Choices for Balancing and Enjoying Your Life

If you are allocating nearly all your time to your job and ignoring your family, your health, your emotions, your own recreation; if you are so hardworking, so disciplined, so "Type A," or so serious that you don't allow yourself to have fun; or if you've forgotten how to have fun, then choose to balance and enjoy your life and make yourself more effective and healthier in the process. This chapter is about how to maintain a balance between success in your job and a happy, healthy personal life. It's about how to improve the overall quality of your life—how to have fun and enjoy life.

The Need to Balance and Enjoy Your Life

You work hard. You put in the long grueling hours. You have minimal time for yourself, let alone for your family and friends. And for what reward? Where do you draw the line? Thomas Horton, recently retired CEO of the American Management Association and author of *What Works for Me: 16 CEOs Talk About Their Careers and Commitments*, raised some very interesting questions in an article in *Success!* magazine (March 1987). He asked: "How dedicated [to your job] must you be? And is there such a thing as being too dedicated?"

In describing his own experience, he said:

> At one time in my career at IBM, I became so committed to succeeding that 14-hour days and 7-day weeks became

my regular schedule. I was not really a workaholic (so I kept telling myself); it was just that the job demands required this dedication. As I dug myself deeper and deeper into the rut I had created, I finally realized how stale I had become. Lacking perspective, I simply plowed ahead, my efforts on the job becoming less and less effective. When I did squarely face the fact that this kind of work behavior represented mismanagement of my time, not to mention of my life, I forced myself to break away and devote some time to my family and myself. Not surprisingly, this made me more productive on and off the job.

Horton said that executives who learn to get away from their work return to it with renewed energy and creativity. That forgetting about your work is exactly what recharges you. And that flashes of insight about your work come when you are least concentrating on it. Horton concluded that if you don't dedicate a part of yourself to yourself, your effectiveness at work will suffer, no matter how dedicated you are to your job.

How dedicated to your job must you be? You need to draw the line somewhere. If you don't take the time to have fun and enjoy life, you are undermining your own effectiveness, health, and happiness. Having fun and enjoying life is not a luxury or something you can keep postponing until it fits into your schedule. It's a requirement for recharging your body, mind, and spirit and for maintaining a proper sense of balance and control in your life. Since you are a busy person, it's something you have to put in your schedule and then do it. It represents the *quality* of your life. Highly successful people know this and lead their lives accordingly.

I remember working with an executive in his office one day. We had been talking for some time. He told me how tired and drained he felt, how he was dragging himself around at work and at home. Then his phone rang. He answered it. Then he started screaming with joy and jumping around. Someone had just given him tickets to an NFL championship game in which his favorite team was playing. Talk about reenergized!

Having fun allows you to experience joy and pleasure. It permits you to become totally absorbed in something that really interests you, something you love, and thereby re-creates and reenergizes you physically, mentally, and spiritually. Just eliminating negative, stressful experiences from your life is not enough. You need to develop and engage in the positive, fun aspects of your life to enjoy it. Lighten up! Have some fun. And some more. And some more.

And for the benefit of you super-hardworking, dedicated types, I'm going to give you permission to have fun. You there, yes you! It *is* okay to have fun. It *is* okay to enjoy life. You have my permission. Now give yourself permission to have fun and enjoy life and just do it.

When to Have Fun and Enjoy Life

One option is *right now*. Since right now is all you have (the past is in the past, the future is in the future), right now is a take charge point for you. Should you have fun and enjoy life in the present moment or not? It's your choice.

If you don't want to have fun right now, when do you plan to have fun? Someday? Well, for most of us dedicated, hardworking types, "someday" rarely or never comes. For many executives, managers, and professionals, "life" is what happens to them while they're busy doing something else.

Have fun every day. A daily dose of fun will do wonders for you, even if it is only a five-minute fun break every now and then throughout the day. Larger doses (a half-day, an evening, a weekend, a week or more) of fun are also highly recommended. Because you are so busy, it is essential that you schedule these larger doses of fun into your life. Put them on your calendar as top priorities because they are—indeed—as important as anything else you do.

Schedule some fun, enjoyable activities for today, some for tomorrow, some for next week, some for next month, and some for the rest of the year. Just being able to look forward to upcoming good times gives you a really good feeling. By scheduling some of your fun ahead of time, you get to enjoy the fun at least three times: in the anticipation, in the actual activity, and afterward in the pleasant memories.

And since having fun makes you more effective, healthier, happier, and a more complete human being, it is a very *productive* thing to do. There! Now all of you who must be productive every minute can have fun, too. The quality of your life will improve dramatically.

Schedule fun and joy into your life. No excuses. There is no guarantee you'll be here tomorrow. I repeat, there is no guarantee you'll be here tomorrow. I know you've heard this before. Maybe this time you'll really hear it. Maybe this time you'll transform your life accordingly. After every funeral, I say to myself, "Life is too short for putting fun times off until "someday." Life is for living, loving, and laughing right now! No one on their deathbed has said, "I wish I spent more time at the office."

As Denis Waitley, world-renowned authority on the psychology of success, says, avoid "Someday Isle." Someday I'll take a vacation. Someday I'll buy that sports car. Someday I'll call that person who means so much to me. Someday I'll read that book. Someday I'll spend some time with my son, with my daughter (Harry Chapin captured this dilemma so beautifully in his song "Cats in the Cradle." If you have it, get it out and listen to it carefully. It'll make you do a few things differently). The problem is that someday never comes and you never do those things. So schedule enjoyable activities in your life. And stick to your schedule. No excuses. No more "Oh, I'll do that *as soon as* I. . . ."

It's Your Choice

Make a deep-down choice right now about how you want to approach the *quality* of your life—your *enjoyment* of life—from now on.

☐ 1. I choose to have fun and really enjoy my life *every day* and to recharge myself in the process. I choose to lead a well-rounded, well-balanced life. As a consequence, I will *enhance* my personal effectiveness, health, and happiness.

☐ 2. I choose not to have fun and not to really enjoy my life every day. I choose not to recharge my batteries by doing fun things. I choose not to lead a well-rounded, well-balanced life. As a consequence, I will *undermine* my personal effectiveness, health, and happiness.

Guidelines for Balancing and Enjoying Your Life

If you chose option 1, here are some specific actions you can take to balance your life and enjoy it more fully.

Check Your Balance

Prepare yourself. This could be a real eye-opener.

1. There are 168 hours in a week. How many of those hours do you spend sleeping? _____ hours.
2. How many hours do you spend on your job (at work, at home, commuting, traveling)? _____ hours.
3. How many hours do you spend with your family? _____ hours.
4. How many hours do you spend on yourself (maintaining or enhancing your body, mind, spirit)? _____ hours.
5. Subtract your sleeping hours from 168. This equals the hours you are awake during a week: _____
6. Calculate the percentage of the awake time you spend on work: ____%; with family: ____%; and on yourself: ____ %.

Are you leading a balanced life? There's no right or wrong allocation of time. It's your call. Ask your body, mind, and spirit. Ask your family. Is your allocation of time in line with the life you truly want as specified in your Command and Control Center? Also see Chapter 5 regarding how to make wise choices about balancing your job, family, and personal life.

Develop an *"I'm Going to Have Fun and Really Enjoy Life"* Mindset

Develop an "I'm going to have fun and really enjoy life" mindset and add it to your collection of powerful, productive mindsets (as discussed in Chapter 10). Consciously choose to enjoy life every day from here on out. By setting your mind to look for and create fun each day, it will. Having fun and enjoying life is more an attitude than anything else. Why not go through life with this kind of attitude? Even at work. The only difference between work and play is your attitude! Can you look at your work as an opportunity to have fun? Can you make it a game, perhaps? It's your choice.

Genuinely Appreciate What You Have

Beware of the "If only I had *x*, then I'd be happy" trap: If only I had more money, a better job, a better figure, another degree, more time, then I'd be happy. This only puts off happiness you could be enjoying right now. And you know what? Once you get whatever it is you wanted, you discover that the happiness it brought you is often short-lived. Before you know it, you start all over again: "If only I had . . . , then I'd be happy."

The only way out of this trap is to realize that the secret to happiness and contentment lies within you. Happiness is a state of mind that you can consciously choose whenever you want. Your happiness does not depend on how much you have but on how much you appreciate what you have! Happiness is not a matter of good fortune or worldly possessions. It comes from appreciating what you do have instead of being miserable about what you don't have.

Reflect periodically on the things with which you have been blessed. This will give you a great feeling instantly. If you can't think of much, take a ride through any large city, read the newspaper, watch TV news, walk through a hospital ward. This is Appreciation 101. Start a list of the basic things you have in your life that you really like having (your good health, your family and friends, clean water or air, enough food, comfortable shelter, nice clothing, sunny days, a blue sky, a talent or skill, the ability to see or hear, the ability to read, walk, or talk).

I like having: _____

_____

_____

_____

If you live in the United States, you probably take a lot for granted. There's a good chance you have far more than the basics. Jot down some of the extras you are happy to enjoy (skis, nice car, nice house, golf clubs, compact disc player, going out to dinner, movies, educational opportunities, books, audiocassettes).

My extras: _____

_____

_____

_____

Disengage

How can you have fun and enjoy life? What can you do to disengage from your job during your workday, in the evening, on weekends, and in larger chunks of time, and get reenergized? I don't know what turns you on, but the possibilities are endless. The answer lies in your answers to these questions: How do you have fun? What gets you excited? What revs up your engine? What makes you really enjoy life?

There will be space in your Personal Effectiveness Plan (discussed in Chapter 14) to write down your answers (so you won't forget how to have fun and enjoy life).

The idea is to find some activities that allow you to disengage from your work. These are activities that truly relax you, that energize you, that allow you to be just you. (Oh, how sweet it is!) Here are some ideas to get your creative juices flowing.

1. *Take short "joy breaks" during your workday.* If you think you always need at least an hour or more to disengage, to do something that's fun, you don't. Ann McGee-Cooper, author of *You Don't Have to Go Home From Work Exhausted!* (see Recommended Resources), suggests you make a list of fun, enjoyable, or energizing things you can do in less than five minutes, so that you can insert a number of "joy breaks" into your day. She recommends reading a poem, listening to a favorite song on your headphones, relaxing with a cup of herbal tea, closing your eyes and visualizing yourself skiing down your favorite slope, playing the perfect hole of golf in your imagination, reading an inspiring book or a joke book (how's your laugh life?), introducing yourself to the new person down the hall, looking at some photographs. Jot your ideas here.

Fun/enjoyable things I can do at work in five minutes or less:

_____

_____

_____

    Then make a list of fun, enjoyable, or reenergizing things you can do in five to thirty minutes (listen to an audiocassette, order a present for a friend from a mail-order catalog, browse through a bookstore on the way home, walk to the café next door for a refreshing drink, plan a surprise for someone you love). McGee-Cooper also suggests you use your prep time in the morning, your commute time, or your lunchtime to do some of the things on your list that are fun and enjoyable in less than thirty minutes. Write your ideas here.

Fun/enjoyable things I can do in five to thirty minutes: _____

_____

_____

_____

2. *Plan to have fun in the evening.* One reason you don't have fun in the evening is that you don't plan to have fun. Perhaps you come home and vegetate in front of the TV. Try planning what fun thing you will do each weekday evening. Consider things like getting out old photo albums and sharing memories, taking a long walk and watching the sunset, giving each other a nice back rub, experimenting with an exotic recipe, teaching your pet a trick, throwing out those old clothes you never wear, learning how to operate your VCR, enjoying a good book with a cup of hot tea and soft music. Jot your ideas here.

Fun/enjoyable things I can do in the evening: _____

_____

_____

_____

3. *Schedule fun for weekends and larger chunks of time.* The key to having more fun and enjoyment in your busy life is to schedule it. Once you have your list of enjoyable activities, schedule them into your life. On weekends and in larger chunks of time, you may want to do some of the fun things you've done in the past. Or you may want to be adventurous and try some new things you have always wanted to try but haven't yet. Make a list of the ten, twenty, or one hundred exciting things you want to do before you die and start doing them. Many successful and happy people do this—Lou Holtz, football coach at Notre Dame, is among them. Start your list here.

Fun/enjoyable things I can do on weekends or in larger chunks of time: _____

_____

_____

_____

_____

4. *Find an interest outside your job.* Look for an activity you can engage in for relaxation and recreation. Normally, the further it is from your occupation the better (recent CEOs of IBM and Exxon were avid bird watchers). Find something you can get totally absorbed in (happiness is being too absorbed in an activity to think about it: woodworking, growing flowers, trout fishing, writing, reading, traveling, being a volunteer cuddler of sick babies, collecting). Try anything that allows you to express your love and caring, anything that makes you say, "Oh, I just love to do that." If you are introverted you will generally (but not always) be reenergized by quiet time and solitary activities away from other people. If you are extroverted, you will usually (but not always) get recharged by being with people. Write your ideas here.

Other nonjob-related interests that contribute to the quality of my life:

Add Quality-of-Life Builders to Your Life

Be sure to include the following quality-of-life builders in your arsenal of revitalizing activities.

1. *Treat yourself right.* Do something nice for yourself every day. This might be treating yourself to your favorite exotic fruit juice one day and a one-hour bubble bath the next.
2. *Schedule some personal development time.* Every day, or at least once a week, use fifteen to thirty minutes for whatever will improve the quality of your life. You might do some creative thinking, work on a self-development project, learn a new language, plan a vacation, or organize your office. Or ask yourself questions like, How can I make myself more effective, healthier, or happier? How can I improve the quality of my life? How can I make my life more fun, more exciting, and more enjoyable?

   This regularly scheduled personal development time can make a huge difference in the quality of your life. The key is scheduling the time and sticking to it. Make it a high priority. If necessary, write it on your calendar as "important meeting with VIP." That Very Important Person, of course, is you.

3. *Do something special for someone else.* Once a day or at least once a week, do something nice that will "make their day" (and yours!). Give and live!

4. *Add music to your daily life and really involve yourself in it.* Express yourself through music. Sing it, play it, dance to it. There is just something special about music that awakens the spirit and makes a person alive. You might want to make a tape of your favorite energizing songs that compel you to move your body, or a tape of your favorite songs for relaxing.

5. *Spend some time just being human.* Be your true self. No roles to play. Take off the mask and just be you. Not a human *doing*, or a human *having*, but a human *being*.

6. *Create special moments* with your spouse, your children. Create memories you will cherish all your life; don't just wait for them to happen. And make time for pure recreation, relaxation, and joy with your family.

7. *Enjoy the present.* Living totally in the present is an exquisite experience. Forget your past. Forget the future. Just savor the current moment and be fully alive in it.

8. *Make contact with nature.* There is something about nature that both grounds us and puts us in contact with a Higher Power at the same time. Discover the beauty and drama in nature. For example, look at the night sky. You'll discover that it is not only beautiful but very much alive with activity. Spend some time with your sky. It's there for you to behold. Enjoy!

Develop a "this is going to be fun" approach to life. Have fun, in big and small doses. Enjoy your life every day.

Recommended Resources

Barlow, Brent. *Successful Marriage.* Eight audiocassettes and workbook. Pleasanton, Calif.: Sybervision, 1986. Learn how to keep romance and excitement alive in your marriage.

Horton, Thomas. *What Works for Me: 16 CEOs Talk About Their Careers and Commitments.* New York: AMACOM, 1989.

Kersey, Katherine. *Successful Parenting.* Eight audiocassettes and workbook. Pleasanton, Calif.: Sybervision, 1986. Learn how to develop competent, confident, and independent children, to help them grow the roots and gain the wings that will enable them to be successful, happy, and productive adults.

McGee-Cooper, Ann. *You Don't Have to Go Home From Work Exhausted!* Dallas: Bowen & Rogers, 1990.

Ziglar, Zig. *Courtship After Marriage.* Book and audiocassette format. Nashville, Tenn.: Thomas Nelson, Publishers, 1990. Learn how to "court your spouse" and fully enjoy your loving relationship.

I CHOOSE TO BALANCE
AND ENJOY MY LIFE
AND RECHARGE MYSELF IN THE PROCESS.

Part Four

Taking Action

This book is about making choices and *taking actions* that will make you far more effective, healthier, and happier. Making wise choices is one thing. Consistently taking action that supports those choices is another.

You have to have a dream to make a dream come true, but dreaming isn't enough. You have to take action!

Chapter 14 shows you how to assemble your complete, life-long Personal Effectiveness Plan and, most important, *how to use it daily*. Chapter 15 shows you how to master your personal effectiveness skills and make them lifelong habits.

14

Your Complete Personal Effectiveness Plan

Putting it all together and using it every single day.

It's time for you to summarize the wiser choices you have made for your life throughout this book on a form called My Personal Effectiveness Plan. The purpose of this written plan is to keep your desired life and your desired approach to life in the forefront of your mind at all times—to keep your dream alive! By completing your Personal Effectiveness Plan, you will know what your primary mission is, the results you want to produce in your job, family, and personal life, what values you have chosen to guide your life, how to create the results you want with greater velocity and joy, and exactly what you can do to keep problems and stress from interfering with your effectiveness, health, and happiness—for the rest of your life!

I suggest you enlarge (copy by hand or photocopy machine) the form on the next few pages so that you have adequate space to write. And keep a blank copy or two on hand for future updates.

Preparing Your Personal Effectiveness Plan

Part One is your Command and Control Center. In it, describe the kind of life you truly want and are willing to put forth the effort to create and list your guiding values. Make sure your Command and Control Center really inspires and empowers you and that it reflects the real, deep-down you. Refer back to the Command and Control Center worksheets you completed in Chapter 5.

Remember that the purpose of Part One, your Command and Control Center, is to create a target that you can lock on to and use to make wise choices throughout each day.

In Part Two, concisely summarize the specific actions—the personal effectiveness skills—you feel will support the Seven Daily Power Choices you made in Chapters 6 through 12. You do not have to include all the supporting actions suggested for the Daily Power Choices; just select those you truly want to use every day to make yourself more effective, healthier, and happier.

In Part Three, complete items 1 to 3, then list the specific ways you will get more enjoyment out of your life (refer to Chapter 13). Include where and when you will do these things. When you are done with this section, take a minute to schedule some of these fun activities into your life right now.

In Part Four, write down specific techniques you have found to be really effective in dealing with specific problems and stressful situations in your job, family, and personal life. These techniques might be based on what's worked well for you in the past or on specific techniques you learned from this book. Over the years to come, keep adding techniques that you find truly helpful.

In Part Five, list some things you know about yourself— personal characteristics—that clearly help you be more effective and some personal characteristics that clearly hinder your effectiveness. Add to this section as you learn more about yourself over the years.

Use It Every Day!

When you have completed your Personal Effectiveness Plan, keep it near you for the rest of your life. Keep it in good shape, perhaps in plastic cover sheets, a folder, or in your time manager. Keep it in your desk drawer, in your briefcase, or wherever it will be handy.

And most important, *use it!* Keep it clearly in mind. Review it every morning to program yourself to create the life you want and to keep you on course. Refer to it when a specific problem or stressful situation arises. Remember your Personal Effectiveness Plan contains proven techniques that will *definitely* make you more effective, happier, and healthier. Use them. You'll be very glad you do. It's your life. It's your choice.

Once you have your Personal Effectiveness Plan completed, you will *know* what kind of life you want to create, how to go about creating it, and how to keep stress, problems, and setbacks from interfering with your creation of that kind of life. Of course, there is always a gap between knowing what to do and doing it. Many of the wise choices and actions you have learned in this book you can implement easily and experience immediate benefits. Other techniques may take more time and effort to learn and to develop into habits. How to do that is the topic of Chapter 15.

My Personal Effectiveness Plan

I am in charge of my life. I am strongly committed to making wise, conscious choices about what I want my life to be like and to taking actions that support those choices and create those results.

Part One: My Command and Control Center

The kind of life I truly want and am willing to put forth the effort to create, and my guiding values.

1. My primary mission in life: _____

_____

_____

2. Other aspects of my dream (the roles and results I want to create in my job, family, and personal life):

Desired roles (prioritized):   Desired results:

_____   _____

_____   _____

_____   _____

_____   _____

_____   _____

_____   _____

3. My guiding values:

_____   _____

_____   _____

_____   _____

_____   _____

_____   _____

Part Two: Seven Daily Power Choices

Personal effectiveness skills that will definitely help me create the kind of life I want. (Be specific, include the what, when, where.)

1. I choose to approach problems in a cool, calm, collected manner every day by:

_____

_____

_____

_____

2. I choose to rest, relax, and rejuvenate my body as needed every day by:

_____

_____

_____

_____

_____

3. I choose to calm my mind, be centered, and think clearly every day by:

_____

_____

_____

_____

4. I choose to be physically tough and full of energy every day by:

_____

_____

_____

_____

5. I choose to be mentally tough, emotionally in control, and action oriented every day by:

_____

_____

_____

_____

_____

6. I choose to communicate in a positive, productive, low-stress manner every day by:

_____

_____

_____

_____

_____

7. I choose to be spiritually strong, resilient, and joyful every day by:

_____

_____

_____

_____

_____

Part Three: Fun Choices for Balancing and Enjoying My Life

1. I choose to use my awake time as follows:

   - On work: _____%
   - On family or social life: _____%
   - On myself: _____%

2. I choose to develop an overall "I'm going to have fun and really enjoy life" mindset by:

_____

_____

_____

3. Appreciation 101. I choose to be happy right now. I will not get caught in the "if only I had *x*, then I'd be happy" trap. My happiness does not depend on how much I have but on how much I appreciate what I have. Here's what I have in my life that I really like having (consider the basics and the extras):

_____

_____

_____

_____

_____

4. Here are some ways that I can disengage from my job, have fun, get energized, and truly enjoy life.

- Fun/enjoyable things I can do during my workday in five minutes or less:

_____

_____

_____

- Fun/enjoyable things I can do during my workday:

_____

_____

_____

- Fun/enjoyable things I can do in the evening:

  _____

  _____

  _____

- Fun/enjoyable things I can do on weekends or in larger chunks of time:

  _____

  _____

  _____

- Other nonjob-related interests that contribute to the quality of my life:

  _____

  _____

  _____

Part Four: Choices for Dealing Effectively With Specific Problems and Stressful Situations in My Job, Family, and Personal Life

JOB-RELATED

Specific problem/situation: Specific technique:

_____   _____

_____   _____

_____   _____

_____   _____

_____   _____

FAMILY AND SOCIAL LIFE

Specific problem/situation: Specific technique:

_____   _____

_____   _____

_____   _____

_____   _____

_____   _____

PERSONAL LIFE

Specific problem/situation: Specific technique:

_____   _____

_____   _____

_____   _____

_____   _____

_____   _____

Part Five: Choosing to Be My Personal Best

I choose to know *myself* so that I can gain more control over my effective and ineffective ways of thinking and behaving—and thereby improve my personal effectiveness!

1. I choose to capitalize on these personal characteristics because they enhance my effectiveness (if not overdone):

_____

_____

_____

2. I choose to guard against these personal characteristics because they can hinder my effectiveness:

_____

_____

_____

3. The kind of work setting and activities that best fit my personality, allow me to be myself, and bring out my personal best:

_____

_____

_____

Making Your Personal Effectiveness Skills Lifelong Habits

Bridging the gap between knowing *what to do and* doing *it!*

The one factor that clearly separates successful people from less successful people is *action*. Just knowing what to do isn't enough. People who are successful *and* healthy *and* happy have developed the habit of *doing* the things that make people successful, healthy, and happy. They may not like to do some of the things that need to be done, but they choose to do them because they know those actions will help produce the results they want most in their lives. Some of the actions may be easy; some hard. In either case, they do them. They consistently and persistently take actions that transforms their dreams into reality.

Four Ways to Take Action

Here are four ways to take action that will get rid of your counterproductive, stress-producing habits and replace them with habits—personal effectiveness skills—that are healthier and more effective in producing what you want most in your life.

1. **Just do it.** One terrific way to make positive changes in your life is to just do it. Just make a decision and do it.
   Some people just decide to stop smoking or stop drinking

and they do it, permanently. Some people just decide to stop eating junk food and they do it, permanently. Some people decide to start exercising, or meditating, or visualizing their success each day and they just do it.

Most often what happens is these people reach a point—a take charge point—where they can no longer tolerate the pain of *not* taking positive action. They feel they must make a wise choice and take action, and they must do it *now!* For example, they get so burned out that they feel they must do something about it *now.* Or they become so frustrated with the way things are going at work or at home that they feel they must learn how to deal with it more effectively before they have a heart attack.

If you have reached a major take charge point in your life where you feel you must take positive, constructive action *now*, just do it! But you don't have to wait until you reach a crisis point. If you are living consciously, your early warning system will let you know when a positive change would make you more effective, healthier, or happier, and you can just do it at that point.

2. **Change your mental associations.** If you haven't quite reached that must-act-now point, then you can help yourself get there.

First, create a strong mental image of the unhealthy or ineffective behavior you want to get rid of and mentally and emotionally associate it with massive pain. For example, say you are a salesperson and you need to do a lot of prospecting by telephone to be successful. But you hate phoning people you don't know so you procrastinate. You find all sorts of reasons why you can't make the phone calls. What you need to do is associate putting off your prospecting calls with massive pain, like you losing your job, your car and home being repossessed, you and your family starving to death.

Then, develop a strong mental image of the healthy or more effective behavior you desire to have and associate it with massive pleasure. For example, associate making lots of excellent prospecting calls every day with massive pleasure like: you making a lot of money, you and your family enjoying several well-earned vacations each year, your professional reputation being the best in the business, you providing your clients with products and services that truly help them be more effective healthier, and/or happier.

Now, repeat these two steps ten, twenty, thirty times or more until you can't stand the thought of putting off your phone calls and you have a very strong desire to make as many calls as you possibly can each day. In fact, you are impelled to make these calls. Strong emotional repetition is the key to success with this method (see Anthony Robbins, *Personal Power*, in Recommended Resources at the end of Chapter 9).

3. **The "So What Am I Going to Do About It" technique.** Another way to get yourself to take action to produce the result you desire is to complete these phrases:

I want _____.
I have _____.
So what am I going to *do* about it? (Make a choice right now and take action.)

For example, I want a relaxed body. I have really tense neck and shoulder muscles. So what am I going to do about it? I'm going to lower my shoulders and do some slow neck rolls to relieve the tension.

4. **Make it happen in twenty-one days.** "Everyone wants to play on a championship team, but no one wants to practice," said Bobby Knight, basketball coach at Indiana University.

How do you turn the skills in your Personal Effectiveness Plan into automatic habits that benefit you for the rest of your life? You do it the way you develop any other habit or skill: practice, practice, practice! Focused effort and repetition are key. The best way to learn this twenty-one-day habit-building, goal-achieving process is to use it.

Plan to succeed. I'd like you to select one personal effectiveness skill (from Chapters 6–13) that you'd like to work on for the next twenty-one days. Now, state your goal on a sheet of paper. Use the SMART acronym to test your goal statement: Is your goal *S*pecific, *M*easurable, *A*ttainable within twenty-one days, *R*eally important to you, and *T*rackable. Make sure your goal statement describes your desired *end result*, is positive, and is stated in the present tense as if you are already doing it; for example, "I'm walking two miles every morning" or "Every day I approach problems instantly in a cool, calm, collected manner." Be sure it's a positive goal you are moving toward rather than a negative situation you are moving away from. Make sure your goal has a specific date for achievement (twenty-one days from now). This is crucial.

Why do you want to work on and achieve this goal? What's in it for you? Write down the positive consequences and pleasure you will receive. Remember you are doing this for yourself; there better be some benefits that are meaningful to you. If not, stop right here; there is no sense taking action on this if there is nothing in it for you. Don't start a self-improvement project just because someone else wants you to do it. Also write down the negative consequences and pain you will avoid by reaching your goal. Then answer the question: How much do I honestly want to accomplish this?

Next, list the obstacles that may hinder your goal achievement (personality characteristics, travel schedule, environmental or cultural factors, family or social factors). Ask yourself how you can deal with each of them effectively. List your ideas or potential actions. Be creative. Do some possibility thinking.

Now, develop a model of effective skill performance. For example, if you want to develop the habit of daily meditation, obtain and write down the specific instructions for the kind of meditation you are going to practice. A good model of effective performance and a good coach can really help you achieve a breakthrough quickly!

Then list any supporting resources you can use to help you achieve your goal. Think broadly here; you may be surprised at the number of resources available to help you. Consider people, organizations, positive cues, relaxation skills, visualizations, affirmations, incentives. It really helps to ask someone you respect to check on your progress periodically (for example, at the end of each week).

One essential supporting item is a scoring or feedback

system. You must keep score each day to monitor and reinforce your progress. Use your daily planner, a calendar, or just draw twenty-one boxes on a piece of paper and put in the dates corresponding to the next twenty-one days. Select performance indicators or measures and choose a daily time for assessing and recording your performance.

Having thought about your goal, potential obstacles, and resources, you are now ready to develop an action plan. What exactly are you going to do before, during, and after the twenty-one-day period? List your action steps in chronological order. Include a date for accomplishing each step. For example, under the heading "Before the Change," write down what you need to do to get ready and when you are going to do it. One thing you need to do is make a scoreboard or decide where you are going to keep score (perhaps in your day planner). You may need to tell key people you want them as helpers. You need to develop or obtain a model of effective performance and line up your other resources. Review Daily Power Choice 5 (Chapter 10) to help you develop the mental toughness you need for success.

Under the heading "During the Change," write down exactly what it is you're going to do each of the twenty-one days to develop your new habit or skill (e.g., center myself each morning, talk with people in a positive, constructive, low-stress manner). Include a way to keep your vision of success in front of you every day (e.g., a daily three-minute visualization session each morning when you can relax and read your goal statement and mentally visualize yourself successfully achieving your goal). Use positive self-talk and images to counteract any goal-sabotaging thoughts or actions during the day. Keep score daily and take a minute to reflect on how you are doing and whether you need to make some adjustments in the goal, your plan, or your commitment.

Under the heading "After the Change," indicate how you are going to celebrate your achievement. How will you reward your successful effort?

Now, when you have finished preparing your action plan, you might proclaim your goal to certain supportive people. If you want to strengthen your commitment, sign your plan of action and have one of them sign also as a witness.

Implement your twenty-one-day plan. Work on your goal every day for twenty-one days straight as planned. If you miss a day, start the twenty-one-day period over again. Practice your new skill every day for twenty-one days. Take action each day. Take action every day. Take action every day. Consistent, persistent action.

Practical Recommendations for Successful Goal Achievement

Work on only *one* significant goal or change at a time. The power of *focused* energy is incredible. Use it! Working on more than one significant goal at a time almost guarantees failure. Trying to develop five personal effectiveness skills at once scatters your energy and attention and is asking too much of yourself. Stay focused for twenty-one days on achieving one valuable goal at a time.

Set a goal that can be achieved in twenty-one days. If your goal is too big, then break it down into bite-size subgoals, each subgoal reachable in twenty-one days. The idea is to have a motivating success experience, not a demotivating experience. Plan on making gradual but steady progress, not on making immediate, gigantic improvements. Easy does it! Your goal should be challenging enough to provide a real benefit yet comfortable enough to you and your current life-style so that you will stick with it and not give up because it was too hard, too difficult to fit in.

Every twenty-one days, set a new goal. Keep turning your new personal effectiveness skills into lifelong habits one skill at a time. Happily accept personal responsibility for improving your personal effectiveness. No excuses. No blaming others. Believe in yourself and embrace a can-do attitude. It's fun and exciting and will provide you with enormous benefits for the rest of your life.

My Challenge to You

You can be very powerful, especially when the going gets tough. You can take on *any* problem, *any* challenge in a cool, calm, collected, positive, productive, and healthy manner.

```
┌────────────────────────────────────────────────┐
│              IT'S YOUR CHOICE!                   │
└────────────────────────────────────────────────┘
```

Just look at any tough situation as a take charge point, an invitation to use your awesome power to make choices and take action. And use your Personal Effectiveness Plan to help you make wise choices and take wise actions. Wise in the sense that your choices and actions *help* you create what you want most in your job, family, and personal life and *help* you be the kind of person you truly want to be.

I hope this book has empowered you and inspired you to take charge of your life—to clarify your dreams and lock on them, to take action that will make your dreams come true, and to take good care of yourself—every single day. And I hope you feel great about yourself. You are great! Go forth with your powerful Personal Effectiveness Plan and, in a cool, calm, and collected manner, . . .

```
┌────────────────────────────────────────────────┐
│        MAKE CHOICES AND TAKE ACTION!             │
└────────────────────────────────────────────────┘
```

Index

CPSIA information can be obtained at www.ICGtesting.com
Printed in the USA
BVOW04s1148300913

332506BV00001B/14/P